W9-BQY-728

LEARNING THROUGH GAMES

A New Approach To Problem Solving

By Elliot Carlson

Public Affairs Press, Washington, D. C.

Published by Public Affairs Press
419 New Jersey Ave., S.E., Washington, D. C. 20003

Printed in the United States of America
Library of Congress Catalog Card No. 69-19771

ACKNOWLEDGEMENTS

Many persons contributed toward this book. They include Allan Brown of William Penn Charter school in Philadelphia; William A. Nesbitt of the Foreign Policy Association; Peter B. Dow of the Education Development Center, Inc., at Cambridge, Mass.; Mrs. Dale C. Farran of the Pennsylvania Advancement School in Philadelphia; Mrs. Sarane Boocock and her staff at Johns Hopkins' Department of Social Relations; Hall T. Sprague of the Western Behavioral Sciences Institute at La Jolla, Calif.; and Harold Guetzkow of Northwestern University.

Others who generously provided materials were Jerry O'Connell of the University of Pennsylvania's Wharton School of Finance and Commerce; David Yount and Paul DeKock of El Capitan High School in Lakeside, Calif.; Richard Wing of the Board of Cooperative Educational Services (BOCES) in Northern Westchester County, N. Y.; Robert C. Shukraft of San Francisco Theological Seminary at San Anselmo, Calif.; Mrs. Barbara B. Varenhorst of the Unified School District in Palo Alto, Calif.; Robert Graves of the University of Chicago; Robert W. Allen of Nova High School in Ft. Lauderdale, Fla.; and the staff of the High School Geography Project in Boulder, Colo.

Many other persons too numerous to mention also contributed various documents and submitted to endless phone conversations. Special thanks are due my wife, Norma, for her particularly helpful comments on the manuscript. I also acknowledge the competent typing of Mrs. Susan Kelly and Mrs. Sara Snyderman.

For the most part, this book is an extension of an article by the author entitled "Games in the Classroom," that appeared in the April 15, 1967, issue of the *Saturday Review*. Also, some of the material in Chapter I appeared in slightly different form in an article by the author in the July 8, 1966, issue of the *Wall Street Journal.*

Despite all the help from others, any errors in the book are the responsibility of the author, who would appreciate corrections.

ELLIOT CARLSON

Philadelphia, Pa.

CONTENTS

Chapter 1

VARIETIES OF GAMING EXPERIENCE

"We are all playing a kind of game in this country today, you know."—*Larry Arrick*

The scene is a plush office in downtown Philadelphia. Around a long walnut table three officers of Bonanza Corp. listen to advice from a well-known consultant who has just ushered the men into his tastefully-appointed quarters. The executives listen attentively as the consultant suggests they shift their advertising from a regional to a national basis. Obviously impressed, they leave without saying more than a word or two.

A few miles away in a musty classroom at the University of Pennsylvania, three officers of Colossal Corp. seem less impressed with their consultant. The men fidget in their chairs as the consultant, a young man just out of school without an office of his own, suggests they shift their advertising from a regional to a national basis. Unconvinced, the executives challenge the consultant's logic and, a few moments later, leave muttering under their breath about bad advice.

Sound like curious behavior for high-powered executives? In fact, the men aren't executives at all. Both Bonanza and Colossal are three-man student teams playing a business game devised by researchers at Penn's Wharton School of Finance and Commerce. The students know they're playing a game, but they don't know the purpose to which this particular game is being put.

Unknown to the young players, several Penn professors in 1966 wanted to know if games could help solve a research problem relating to the effectiveness of business consultants. Specifically, the professors wanted to know whether the relative prestige of consultants would explain the differences in the client's acceptance of the proffered advice—even if it were bad.

So the professors set up two make-believe companies and exposed them to two consultants—one of which was surrounded by the trappings of success while the other appeared almost seedy. Both consultants, however, gave exactly the same advice; some of it was good, some bad. Sure enough, the "high prestige" consultant had the students eating out of his hand. They tended to swallow his suggestions even though they were warned some of them might be bad. The "low prestige" consultant fared less well; indeed, students rejected his advice even when it was good.

As a result of the experiment, Jeremiah J. O'Connell, assistant professor of industry at Penn, was able to generalize that a consultant's prestige may be a commanding factor in whether or not his advice is accepted.[1] This particular experiment was unique, but it provides a bizarre example of the many uses to which a variety of new problem solving games are being put in schools and laboratories across the country.

Perhaps to most people the word games still conjures images of children's antics and, at best, various forms of parlor frivolity. But in recent years the word has taken on an altogether different meaning for educators, businessmen and even government policymakers concerned with how people, youngsters and oldsters alike, learn things. Or, more precisely, can be encouraged to learn things, from problem-solving strategies to intellectual concepts. For researchers from a growing number of fields strategy games, many of which resemble their parlor precursors, have educational possibilities that only in the last few years have been discovered, tested and applied. Despite controversy over their educational effects, the new-fangled exercises today are being used for a bewildering array of purposes by government agencies, businesses, hospitals, labor unions and every kind of school (including seminaries).

Development of strategy games for this wide variety of uses has taken place in little more than 10 years. But there is, to be sure, nothing new about gaming itself. War games, for example, are as old as gladiators and jousting knights, who used them to develop alternative tactics and strategies. Authorities have traced war gaming back to chess, which probably originated in ancient India. The early Indian game consisted of elephants, horses, chariots and infantry. As one historian has noted, "pieces used in the original Hindu game represented the same four elements of an army, and the supporting frame of the chessboard employed today symbolizes the wall of a fortified city." [2]

Even with its many limitations as a war game, military men found that the spirit of chess nevertheless approached that of war. So it was that military officers lacking opportunities to practice their trade except in times of war, developed war games out of their experiences with chess. Perhaps the first such adaptation of chess was the "King's Game," or "military chess," developed in 1644 for the Prussian general staff. The game, aimed at giving cadets a vehicle for the study of war and maneuver, involved 14 varieties of moves for 30 pieces on each side: a king, officers, chancellors, heralds, couriers, chaplains, adjutants, bodyguards, halberdiers and private soldiers (the pawns).[3]

It wasn't until after the Napoleonic wars, which saw massed national armies and rapid maneuver, that war games were moved off the chess board and made more realistic. In 1824, another soldier (also a Prussian), transferred gaming to maps and, as one authority puts it, "adapted war gaming to the simulation of actual military operations." [4] The game, which later became the prototype of much modern war gaming, included leaden troop pieces made to scale and colored to indicate opposing sides. The game also included scales of ranges and distances, dividers and dice. The key to the game, however, was the umpire, who, like his counter-part in some modern games, judged what impact decisions made by competing players had on the game situation.

Later, political and logistical factors were worked into military games, resulting in large brochures describing the political setting of each combatant. By 1860, military games had all the elements of modern exercises: the notion of time, detailed simulation of activities, and awareness of pertinent environmental forces. At that time games were conducted by an umpire and a clerical staff with the aid of a rule book, which defined the elapsed time allowed for each move, what decisions were to be made and other matters.

Soon afterwards there developed another movement to make games more "realistic." To this end, gamesters worked into the exercises reams of data gathered on past wars, which required participants to master huge rule-learning books before they could play the game. This burdensome requirement led to the creation in 1874 of a new school of war gaming referred to as free *kriegspiel* which relied completely upon experienced umpires with no rule book.[5] Gamesters inside this movement attempted to formulate teams with special skills to eliminate the need for logistics and political data. Consequently war games came to be identified as either free or rigid, depending upon the role of the umpire.[6]

Put simply, "free" games tend to be those that rely heavily on the subjective judgment of a human umpire, who evaluates the outcome of moves made by the players. In some free games the umpire also may rule out moves on grounds of their supposed implausibility. In one such game developed at the Massachusetts Institute of Technology the umpire also acts as "nature," inserting new "facts," passing on confidential information from one party to another, or leaking rumors of anticipated team moves in order to speed up the action or lend an air of suspense.

In "rigid" games, the outcomes tend to be pre-determined; they can either be looked up in a rule book or, in the case of many modern games, calculated by a computer, which is programmed with certain cause-and-effect formulas. Some games involve a mix of these two approaches.

Before the 19th century closed, war games spread in one form or another to England, France, Austria-Hungary, Russia, Italy, Turkey, Japan and the United States. In this century, the Germans used military games as a means for rehearsing their 1918 spring offensive in World War I; and in World War II preliminary studies based on war games were used by Germans in planning the invasions of France in 1940, of the Ukraine in 1941, and the potential invasion of England which never did take place.[7] Both American and Japanese military planners used war games, although with mixed results, prior to and during World War II. Fleet Admiral Chester W. Nimitz declared in 1960: "The war with Japan had been re-enacted in the game rooms . . . by so many people in so many different ways that nothing that happened during the war was a surprise—absolutely nothing except the Kamikaze tactics toward the end of the war . . ."[8]

What accounted for the proliferation of war games? In his book, "The Crisis Game," Sidney Giffin observes that war games have never represented a means of arriving at those new concepts of organization and tactics required by the advent of new weapons. But he adds that games have provided a "useful means of inculcating concepts already formed, of emphasizing rules and planning factors, and of affording practice in the field of decision-making." War gaming, however, was given tremendous impetus after World War II with the advent of computers, which provided instant feedback on the consequences of decisions made by the players.

At the same time, games were called upon to solve far more complicated "war games" than ever before. Indeed, the making of models for various types of gaming connected with the operations of military forces has become big business. The Raytheon Co., for one, has developed a computer simulation of cold war and limited war for the Joint War Games Agency of the Joint Chiefs of Staff. As Giffin explains it:[9]

"An ambitious attempt has here gone into gaming political, economic and psychological events, among other things, for as many as 39 nations simultaneously. The designers do not claim predictive capabilities for their model, known as TEMPER. They hope, however, to achieve good qualitative results on the basis of alternative assumptions, providing material for further analysis."

Gaming also has become one of the favorite research techniques of the so-called "think tanks." In the early 1950's the Rand Corp.'s Mathematics Division developed a military-political game called Cold War, and in 1954, Rand's Social Science Division put together a slightly different game called Political Exercise, aimed at "gaming out" situations of national and international conflict. The Massachusetts Institute of Technology in the early 1960's developed, among other games, a series of "arms control" exercises for the Institute for Defense Analyses. The Hudson Institute, under Herman Kahn, has used games to develop what might be called "fictional world futures." Unlike most politico-military games, which are concerned with the short-term, Kahn's games attempt to deal with possible situations ten or more years in the future.

There seems little question that games have become almost indispensable to military planners. Since 1951, the Joint Chiefs of Staff, through the Joint War Games Agency, have used a series of "politico-military desk games." Details of games have been kept largely secret, but one unclassified Pentagon document is, to say the least, enthusiastic about the exercises:[10]

"[Politico-military] desk games are different from most games employed in operations research, particularly as they are played in the Joint Staff. In the Joint War Games Agency, these games are used to assist in the analysis of national objectives, policies, plans, programs and organization by illuminating future possible contingencies. They are not intended to be predictive. They are played by top level officials from the White House, State and Defense Departments, and the Services for the following benefits: Simulated crises environment; realistic communications obstacles; exercise of command, control and intelligence systems; build interagency and interechelon rapport; point up weak spots in coordination, etc.; provide 'feel' for cold war 'bargaining,' negotiation, and escalation processes; broad overview for specialists; cross-fertilize ideas between agencies."

Games are vulnerable to abuses, however, and sometimes are used for purposes never intended by their designers. A case in point is provided by the Total War Research Institute of Japan's wartime government, whose military clique apparently was too divided to submit to the unbiased rules of the properly conducted strategy game. Rather than take gaming seriously, some Japanese war planners viewed the exercises as instruments by which they could make their will prevail over that of dissident colleagues. It's conceivable that Japan's curious use of strategy games contributed to that country's overconfidence immediately prior to the invasion of Midway.

Extensive politico-military gaming preceded formation of the huge Japanese armada that was to converge on the remote Pacific island. During these mock operations, the Japanese assault on Midway was carried out with ease. But this was largely attributable to the fact that Admiral Ugaki, the pro-invasion officer who presided at the war games, frequently set aside rulings made by the more objective umpires. Hoping to stifle objections that could be raised against the Midway venture, Ugaki on one occasion changed all verdicts on the anticipated air fighting and altered them in favor of Japan.

In his biography of Admiral Yamamoto, who conceived and engineered the attack on Midway, John Deane Potter describes one such war game in which the Japanese fleet was bombed by American aircraft while its own planes were in the air attacking Midway. One umpire, an air staff officer, ruled there had been nine enemy hits on the Japanese carriers. Two carriers, Akagi and Kaga, were listed as sunk. But Admiral Ugaki reduced the number of hits to three, with only Kaga being sunk and Akagi slightly damaged.[11] In short, Ugaki was using games to argue a set of predetermined convictions rather than investigate the possible reactions of an enemy to a course of action.

With today's far more complex games, in which computer calculations often replace the subjective judgments of the individual umpire, Admiral Ugaki would have had a much harder time tinkering with the outcome of the game. But there were other difficulties with games that plagued—and to some extent still do—military planners. In her analysis of the Pearl Harbor debacle, Roberta Wohlstetter observes that both American and Japanese games consistently misread the intentions of their adversaries. She comments:[12]

"This inability to imagine enemy psychology and tactics is, of course, a flaw inherent in most war games; the strategies are as good as the players and, on the whole, are typical of the players rather than of their identities in the game. The American decision makers, it has been noted, were rather poor at imagining Japanese intentions and values. It should be said that the Japanese themselves had essential difficulties . . . with projecting American responses to Japanese acts. Most unreal was their assumption that the United States, with ten times the military potential and a reputation for waging war until unconditional victory, would after a short struggle simply accept the annihilation of a considerable part of its air and naval forces and the whole of its power in the Far East."

Despite the rich history of war gaming, it wasn't until 1956 that the American Management Association, spurred by the growing availability of computers, put together the first widely known management training game. According to an AMA official, computers brought "simulations closer to reality by increasing the number of variables that could be handled." It wasn't long before the exercises worked their way into the university and business communities. Indeed, "they were status symbols in many executive suites," recalls one executive who later became disillusioned with the strange new exercises. Adds one AMA official: "Our development triggered a fad in which games were a flossy new product around which some companies tried to build entire training programs."

On the heels of high expectations came disillusionment with games. But more recently there has been a renewal of interest in management training games along more moderate lines. Today few if any companies expect games by themselves to solve long-standing management training problems. But even while generating more modest expectations, they are more widely used than ever. According to some authorities, about 200 companies today use games to supplement the pamphlets, lectures and case studies on which most management training and employe indoctrination courses are based. The exercises may simulate the problems of running an industry, a company or a particular corporate department. Currently they are being used for everything from teaching executives investment strategies and collective bargaining techniques to boosting employe morale. Players come from production lines, executive suites and all points in between.

What makes games effective, authorities agree, is their peculiar ability to motivate. "They work because they get the total involvement of the participant," says John W. Cogswell, who directs management training programs for American Telephone & Telegraph Co. "Games liven up a training program," adds Richard Rosen of Abt Associates, Inc., a Cambridge, Mass., based maker of games for companies, unions, schools and government agencies. "They also allow an employe to participate in decision-making situations much earlier in his career than he usually would be able to."

A look at a few business games illustrates the wide variety of uses to which they can be put. At Proctor & Gamble Co., for example, employes several times each year are asked to break up into teams of four and spend six hours playing VENTURE, a company game. New sales personnel, management trainees and clerks and production workers who have been with Proctor & Gamble for at least five years play in each of the company's 14 plants and its Cincinnati home office. The game puts company employes in the shoes of a simulated management team running a firm that makes cake mix or detergents. It gives them "the opportunity to see the total decision-making process involved in running a business," says a Proctor & Gamble spokesman. The company claims VENTURE gives hourly workers a new appreciation for management problems along with the realization that their own jobs are important to the company's operations.

Boeing Co. makes slightly different use of games, aiming them at managers as they rise through company ranks. Most every year at Boeing about 1,000 employes in line for management jobs play Operation Feedback, a game that simulates difficulties they may face as managers. Operation Suburbia pulls the concern's middle-management men away from the aircraft industry to wheel and deal in real estate speculation, an exercise designed to show them the importance of planning on a long-range basis, organizing their work and cooperating with other executives working toward similar goals. Top managers play Operation Interlock, a game that closely resembles Boeing's own business and highlights the company's particular problems.

With a game called FAME, International Business Machines Corp. carries computer involvement a step further than most business games, which use machines to calculate the effect of players' decisions on the overall situation. Rather than rely on the computer merely as a kind of umpire, FAME players use the machine to analyze problems and alternatives before deciding what to do. Most every year dozens of IBM managers play FAME at IBM's Sands Point, New York, management school, while a few miles away in Poughkeepsie executives of companies using IBM computers play FAME to "learn what a computer is and how mangaement science techniques can be applied to their companies," says Kenneth Powell, IBM's manager of education research.

By no means are all business games as strictly quantitative as the Boeing and IBM games, which chiefly involve decisions about how much to spend or invest. Many business games simply try to stretch executives' imaginations and improve their abilities to get along with people. One such game is that played annually by about 25 Sun Oil Co. executives, who divide themselves into fictional companies manufacturing and selling waffle irons. To add realism and pleasure to the game, teams issue annual reports, one of which was recently entitled, "Flounders Waffle Iron Corp., Flip Your Waffles with Flounders—You Will Smell the Difference." The game also shuffles participants into unfamiliar roles by assigning production experts to sales jobs and vice versa.

"We want our managers to be more than specialists," said James W. Porter, Sun's personnel development director. "We want them to have empathy for other functions and understanding of the total management job. Games enable a player to make mistakes and fall on his face without actually being penalized."

Games such as Sun's, which primarily concern themselves with the intricacies of personal relationships, have spread to different areas of business and sometimes outside the executive suite altogether. An example is Public Relations, recently developed by Abt Associates for the American Institute of Banking. The idea of the game is to teach managers of small and medium-sized banks how to allocate advertising funds without excessively alienating those media receiving only a small chunk of the advertising pie, yet whose business may be important to the bank. The game can get nasty since participants playing the role of media people can shift bank deposits on the basis of how the bankers treat them. Thus, the game stresses bargaining—and what game-makers call "the principle of reciprocity." "The job of the banker is to make a decision that's best, given the things that are out of his control," says an Abt official.

Industrial Relations Counselors, Inc., a New York based, non-profit research and management training group, has put together a game for hospitals designed to help administrators get better cooperation from staff members by acquainting them with the problems and priorities of other departments in the hospital. In bargaining sessions the "department heads" establish priorities of need, but when emergencies develop they must "wheel and deal" to balance the service demand of others with their own needs. Later teams are scored on how well they met these competing demands and handled inter-departmental relations.

Inter-personal maneuvering also is a key element of a collective bargaining game developed by IRC. In the game executives divide themselves into labor-management teams and negotiate contracts the way actual teams would in real life. While the game can be used to help introduce neophyte labor relations men to the collective bargaining process, "most participants are personnel or industrial relations people seeking an expanded awareness of the pressures involved in such negotiations," says an IRC official. "They discover the problems of reaching a compromise and learn why the company takes a certain bargaining position."

Unions also play games. One game-maker says it developed a strategy game for an industrial union that resembles a counter-insurgency game the concern had earlier developed for the Defense Department. For the purpose of the game, labor and management "representatives" compete for the support of unorganized workers much in the same way insurgents and government, in the Defense Department game, compete for the support of uncommitted villagers. "Labor union organizing problems are similar to those faced by insurgents," says the game-maker.

While it denies using any games such as this one, the United Auto Workers does use them for various purposes. The union recently considered a simulation that would deal with the ticklish problem of intra-union relationships. "The problem has to do with younger members just entering the union who aren't familiar with UAW history," says a UAW spokesman. "The game would place old members in the role of new ones and vice versa to sensitize our staff to this new problem."

What participants actually get out of the exercises is a matter of hot debate among gamers. While even critics agree that some kind of learning goes on during games, they also point out there is no evidence that players learn anything from them that could not have been learned from conventional methods. For this reason Travelers Insurance Co., for one, discontinued games altogether after using them in 1960. "Games generate great enthusiasm among managers, but the end result is that they get more concerned with who wins than they do with what the game is trying to teach them," complains Andrew H. Souerwine, director of management conferences for Travelers.

Defenders of simulations reply that the learning spurred by gaming is often too intangible to be measured; they contend that games convey a sensitivity to the interplay of forces involved in decision-making or bargaining that other teaching methods can't match. In some cases executives claim that the learning effects of games are quite concrete. An official of Nationwide Insurance claims that the concern's managers, after playing a company-designed game involving various technical charts, "are better able to understand technical data and deal with the rapid flow of information coming to them." One result of a game played by managers at McKesson & Robbins, Inc., is that "when the men go back to their divisions we find that in letters and conversations they do more talking about return on investment rather than just sales and profits," says the firm's spokesman. The company feels that the game has real meaning for managers since promotions are based in part on how well their divisions do in terms of return on investment, which is one criteria for success in the game.

Whatever the learning effects of games, a subject that will be returned to more fully later, there's no question that they are proliferating and spreading far beyond their original confines. Most noticeably in schools. Indeed, it is in the schools where strategy games are most varied and where, ultimately, their use may prove most rewarding. A growing number of schools are finding that various problem-solving games can be helpful in teaching everything from mathematics and business administration to international relations.

Hastening entry of the sometimes controversial games into secondary and elementary schools is mounting teacher dissatisfaction with old-fashioned textbook approaches to course material. Schools in Baltimore, Philadelphia and elsewhere have found that the exercises can help motivate slow learners. And grade schools in northern Westchester County, New York, working under a U.S. Office of Education grant, have designed games to teach sixth graders the economic problems of an emerging nation and the operation of a retail toy store.

On the university level, the same spirit of innovation is infecting a growing number of graduate schools of business, where some educators contend games may remedy a deficiency in those curriculums overlooking that decision-making occurs in a context of conflict. In the early 1960's, the University of Chicago's Graduate School of Business introduced a game reflecting the workings of the international trade system. About the same time the Harvard Business School introduced a game for first-year graduate students simulating a consumer goods industry. In 1966, the University of Pennsylvania's Wharton School of Finance and Commerce introduced a similar game. In all, some fifty university business schools make use of management games, about double the number in 1963, according to one estimate. Business schools by no means monopolize games, however. At Northwestern University, the University of Michigan, and a sprinkling of other colleges, political science students play a game called Inter-Nation Simulation (INS) which supplements courses in international relations.

The emergence of games in the classroom can only be understood in terms of new developments in educational theory and a trend towards curriculum reform sweeping many areas of education. One such development, which underlies the "new math" and the "new social studies," is the view that teaching should be concept-oriented. Advocates of games as teaching aids claim that concepts can best be grasped—intellectually as well as viscerally—through various problem-solving exercises. Hall Sprague, director of the Western Behavioral Science Institute (WBSI), a La Jolla, Calif. based research group which has pioneered in simulation, argues that games bring concepts down to what he calls "gut-level." Researchers contend that in such international games as INS, WBSI's Crisis, and Dangerous Parallel, a game put together recently by the Foreign Policy Association, the concept of balance of power is not simply learned by rote but is actually experienced.

For James S. Coleman, professor of Social Relations at Johns Hopkins University, the rise of educational games involves an extensive critique of the high school in American society and the place of the adolescent in that society. To Coleman the American high school, established in a simpler time when only a small proportion of adolescents continued beyond grade school, has failed to come to grips with the tougher problems of the mid-20th century. He notes that today high schools are expected to prepare young people from all walks of life for a far more complex and impersonal society.

Coleman contends the conditions that underpinned the 19th century high school no longer abide. In schools where few students are college bound, he suggests "there is little motivation, and the teen-age culture encourages its members to defy discipline and to hold down effort in scholastic directions, and diverts energies into exciting and autonomous activities that interfere with the school's task."[13] And even in those few schools where students are highly motivated, the professor notes that "they are no more willing to accede to the authority of adults, and instead turn to one another for their direction and their rewards." Consequently, he argues that the structure of secondary education is appropriate neither to college bound youths nor to those students who will at most finish high school.

To Coleman and his Johns Hopkins colleague, Sarane S. Boocock, secondary education today has three structural defects that make various problem-solving games a plausible alternative to some teaching practices. What are these defects? Perhaps the most fundamental, according to the two researchers, is that secondary schools teach for a long-distance future. This view holds that young children, even unintelligent ones, can learn to speak a language at an early age because doing so involves their ability to get along in their immediate environment with friends, parents and others. But older children allegedly run into trouble when they are taught in school those skills that will enable them to get along in a *future* environment. The problem, apparently, is that while the young person will need many of these later, this later need provides little or no motivation for the present. Coleman and Boocock comment:[14]

"The greatest problem, then, appears to be due to a mismatching of time. The child is being taught for a future whose needs have not yet impressed themselves upon him; hence, he sees little need to focus his energies upon learning. He is, moreover, being taught for a future that is different from that his familiar adults are presently experiencing. The rapidity of social change induces an uncertainty about what skills will be relevant in it."

A second structural defect in high schools, according to the two researchers, lies in the enforced, involuntary character of the curriculum. They contrast this curriculum with the scholarship required in graduate schools, where students are rewarded for spectacular achievement. But high schools are charged with providing students with little motivation to carry on in a direction as far as they can. Instead, students must operate inside fixed limits that make a high school education consist of little more than "completing assignments." This comes at a time, say Coleman and Boocock, when adolescents are looking less to adults and more to each other for rewards. As a result, teen-agers tend to spurn the adult-imposed curriculum and seek out voluntary activities, such as athletics, that permit high rewards for spectacular achievement.

A final defect, according to Coleman and Boocock, is the dual role of the teacher as both teacher and judge. The problem here, they say, is that the teacher must teach students as well as give them grades that can greatly affect the students' futures. This, the argument goes, often leads students to develop attitudes toward teachers that can interfere greatly with learning: hostility, servility, alienation, and other reactions to an authority figure.

Proponents of games allow that no instructional tool can fully overcome these defects. Just the same, some gamesters contend that to a certain extent games can alter the structure of education in ways that go some distance to meet these problems. Consequently, Johns Hopkins' Department of Social Relations since the early 1960's has been developing what it calls "games with simulated environments." Financed by a series of Carnegie Corporation grants, the department has developed a Life Career game in which a boy or girl must weave his or her way through the occupational structure, political games, legislative games, consumer games and others aimed at providing the adolescent with practice in dealing with those large institutions which make up the adult world.

According to Coleman and Boocock, the values of such games arise from several sources:[15]

"First, and perhaps most important, they bring the future into the present, allowing the child to play roles in a large differentiated society of which he otherwise gets hardly a glimpse. Thus they surround a child with an environment which is artificial for the present, but realistic for the future. His academic task is not to carry out assignments, but to 'survive' in this complex environment. In playing a management game, a child is forced to turn to economic texts not to get a grade, but for economic survival in this complex environment. In a consumer game (involving allocation of income in the face of credit financing, advertising pressures, and unpredictable events), a boy or girl must learn both economics and mathematics, as well as the necessity to defer gratifications. More generally, a boy or girl will be able to play at those roles that he must play in earnest once he becomes an adult, and enters the complex modern society of adults. In so doing, he learns both the intellectual skills relevant for those roles, and the moral traits—that is, the traits which schools presently attemp to inculcate under the general label of 'citizenship education.' "

Secondly, games are considered valuable because of their strange ability to motivate, and finally, because they are self-judging. That is, the outcome of the game decides the winner, and a player knows that he has won or lost by his own actions. This, at least in theory, enables the teacher to escape from the role of judge, and return to his original function, that of teacher or helper for the student.[16]

Central to the Johns Hopkins critique of the large public high school is the role in that school of athletic competition, whose participants, many studies have shown, tend to monopolize school's social rewards. At the same time, non-athletic scholars tend to be ridiculed as "curve raisers" or "grinds." As a result, many critics have charged that athletic programs drain student energies away from the school's basic educational tasks.

The real problem, according to Coleman, is that the academic victories of the brilliant student are purely personal ones, often at the expense of his classmates, who are forced to work harder to keep up with him.[17] Unlike the efforts of the athlete, those of the outstanding student seldom bring prestige or glory to the high school. Coleman believes high schools never will be able to perform their educational functions unless there is a change in the allocation of rewards and prestige inside what he calls the "adolescent society." But he argues this can't be done by doing away with all forms of scholastic competition which, he claims, is a basic energizing and motivating device.

In his book *The Adolescent Society*, Coleman suggests that schools consider substituting intergroup competition in academic areas for the interpersonal competition for grades which currently exists. In Coleman's view, this substitution would require dropping the notion that each student's achievement must be continually evaluated or "graded" in every subject.[18] Instead the change would make such evaluations infrequent and subsidiary to contests and games both within the school and between schools. The professor notes, however, that the change from "interpersonal to intergroup" competition would require the creation of new forms of competition: intellectual games, problems, group and individual science projects, scholastic fairs and other activities.

Through such contests, the brilliant student would have, at least in theory, an opportunity to bring "glory to the school" much in the same way the athlete does. Thus, the argument goes, academically inclined students would be accorded the same social rewards, encouragement and respect currently enjoyed by athletes. The important thing, according to Coleman, is the general principle that "motivations may be sharply altered by altering the structure of rewards, and more particularly that among adolescents, it is crucial to use informal group rewards to reinforce the aims of education rather than impede them."[19]

Whether games can actually achieve such results, or whether such reliance on games is even desirable, are open questions. There is, in fact, evidence that some of the original claims for educational games were, like those for management games a few years earlier, excessive. Indeed, some educators already have scaled down their expectations for the strategy exercises. Nevertheless, a number of schools are pushing ahead with academic games programs along the lines advanced by Coleman (how one Florida junior-high school has made particularly inventive use of games will be discussed later).

A question that raises itself is why games are intrinsically motivating. To suggest an answer it is necessary to allude to the growing literature on the role of "play" in the formation of both societies and individual personalities. To anthropologist Johan Huizinga the play-element is a "culture-creating force" without which real civilization cannot exist.[20] Philosopher George Herbert Mead has contended that it is through play, with its role-taking activities, that the child learns to relate to the outside world, what Mead calls "the other." To Mead the difference between play and games is that in games, with their rules and regulated procedures, the child must have the attitude of all the others involved in that game. Thus, Mead suggests that games are illustrations of the social situation out of which a fully developed personality arises.[21]

More recently, Jean Piaget has observed that the simple games children play, such as marbles, appear to be crucial means for learning about and experimenting with life. According to some of his interpreters, games constitute a kind of introduction to life—an introduction to the idea of rules, which are imposed on all alike.[22]

It is evident that strategy games attempt to tap some of the same resources and creative energies called into being by the more spontaneous forms of play described by Piaget and Mead. An economist has this to say about games and motivation:[23]

"Most human motives tend on scrutiny to assimilate themselves to the game spirit. It is little matter, if any, what we set ourselves to do; it is imperative to have some objective in view, and we seize upon and set up for ourselves objectives more or less at random—getting an education, acquiring skill at some art, making money, or what-not. But once having set ourselves to achieve some goal it becomes an absolute value, weaving itself into and absorbing life itself. It is just as in a game where the concrete objective—capturing our opponents' pieces, carrying a ball across a mark, or whatever it may be—is a matter of accident, but to achieve it is for the moment the end and aim of being."

The rise of educational games, then, is a product of a complex of factors: The long rich history of war gaming, the development of computers, and quite recently, the growing appreciation by educators of a link between play and learning. Yet strategy games would not have reached their present stage of sophistication without what is known in scholarly circles as "game theory," the outgrowth of the work of two economists in the 1930's.[24]

Before the advent of game theory, most games for training were war games with two opponents. The vocabulary of game theory provided the final catalyst to allow complex games to be developed in a variety of environments, according to one devotee of games.[25] In the 1930's game theorists demonstrated that all forms of competitive behavior, be it economic, military or social, could be construed as a process of strategy development and implementation. According to game theorists, such strategies are defined by a series of decisions in an uncertain environment over an extended period of time. In short, game theory made it possible for many different opponents to compete in a game, and to do so on many different levels of competition.

Game theory led naturally to the development of simulations for theory-building and predictive purposes in international relations, business administration and other areas. Such application of games is beyond the scope of this small volume, which, happily for the author, will be confined almost entirely to the variety, uses and effects of games developed for teaching purposes.

CHAPTER 2

BUSINESS GAMES: MAIN STREET TO LIECHTENSTEIN

"All coherent thinking is equivalent to playing a game according to a set of rules."—*Arthur Koestler*

What is a game? The question is surprisingly troubling, since the word is often used interchangeably with more scholarly terms like simulation and role-playing. Games, or simulations, may involve some form of role-playing, but role-playing by itself, in which a child plays "doll house" or "soldier," does not add up to what experts would call a game. One gamemaker observes that "role plays differ from games in that the former may have more determined outcomes and may not be competitive." [1]

Some of the same experts also insist on distinguishing games from simulations. According to Clark C. Abt, "war games are sometimes confused with models and simulations, since sometimes models are 'gamed,' games are modeled, and both models and games are simulated. A *game* is any contest played according to rules and decided by skill, strength, or apparent luck. A *model* is a representation—actual or theoretical—of the structure or dynamics of a thing or process. A *simulation* is an operating imitation of a real process." [2]

Complicating the search for a definition of games, and/or simulations, is the fact that the same words are often applied to exercises and experiments that are only superficially similar. Some pedants, for example, reserve the word simulation for those occasions during which computers are the only "players." Such simulations are usually used by physical and natural scientists who need problem-solving methods with a high degree of precision. Thus, scientists describe as "a simulated environment" the wind tunnel in which they place a model of an airplane wing for controlled observation. Also, medical doctors simulate diseases with computer-manipulated variables to isolate causes and, hopefully, find cures. The National Aeronautics and Space Administration has used simulations for a variety of purposes.

Purists often dismiss as a mere "game" any exercise that is manual (man-played) or man-machine (in which players obtain their information from data provided by a computer). Gamesters who appropriate the word "simulation" for their exercises do so on grounds that games may, like the wind tunnel, involve a miniaturization or reduced form of reality. While such games do not attempt to replicate reality with the exactitude of a wind tunnel, they do attempt to isolate the key variables involved in a social process. Strategy games, then, purport to be simplified models in which students play roles in the process or system modeled. At the same time, games involve a payoff in which there is a "winner," although the criteria for determining winning varies from game to game.

At Johns Hopkins' Department of Social Relations, which has developed what it calls "games with simulated environments," the two words are used almost interchangeably. To the department's James Coleman, a social simulation game "is a game in which certain social processes are explicitly mirrored in the structure and functioning of the game. The game is a kind of abstraction of these social processes, making explicit certain of them that are ordinarily implicit in our everyday behavior."[3] How Johns Hopkins has translated these notions into games like Family, Life Career and others will be discussed later.

How the many variables of a process can be brought together into a single exercise is perhaps best illustrated by management training games, among the most complex of all games used in the classrooms. Three that will be looked at in some detail are the Harvard Business School Management Game, the Carnegie Tech Management Game and INTOP, an international trade game played at the University of Chicago's Graduate School of Business.

These three man-machine games can be defined in terms not unlike those used for Abt's war games and Coleman's social simulations. Harvard's James L. McKenney, associate professor of business administration, defines a management game as "a competitive mental activity wherein opponents compete through the development and implementation of an economic strategy." According to McKenney, the three basic components of a simulation include an abstraction of an economic environment, or a *model;* or a series of rules for manipulation of the model, *simulation;* and a set of rules which govern the activity of the participants in relation to the simulation, or *game.*[4]

How do such games work? In practice business games tend to resemble each other. As the typical business game gets underway, players huddle over charts and sheets containing background data on their fictional concerns. Then the team makes a decision, usually expressed in dollar terms, on the amount of money to be spent on production, marketing, research or some other area of the concern's business. The impact of these decisions on a mythical market and, consequently, on the other "companies" in the market, is calculated by the umpire, which, in the case of business games, is generally a computer programmed with certain cause-and-effect formulas. The umpire changes the situation in accordance with the players' decisions. Reports are issued and then the participants, armed with new information, make a new set of decisions, a process that goes on for a predetermined set of "quarters."

In the HBS game, the competition between players is governed by the economic model, which is a facsimile business environment whose basic design the participants cannot control. The participants do, however, influence the economic development of the mythical environment by their choice of strategies in the game. In economic terms, the model represents the demand function for an industry and the mechanism for determining the quantity of production given a schedule of resource allocations in the form of dollar budgets.

The model consists of a series of equations representing a consumer market, a financial market, a productive capacity for each firm in the game, and an accounting model which extracts cost and tabulates data for each firm. In the HBS game, the word simulation refers to that portion of the game in which this economic abstraction is manipulated in accordance with a set of rules. An example of such a rule would be, "Select the minimum of inventoried material, allocated labor, and prior plant capacity as the production output for the decision period." The game's rules prescribe the number, form and timing of a series of economic decisions for managing a facsimile firm.

Purpose of the game, which involves about five graduate student "executives" representing six or seven competing firms in a fictional appliance industry, is almost breathtakingly ambitious. The game is aimed at developing the student's ability in problem solving, including discovering, analyzing and weighing the significant factors of a business problem, and deciding on a course of action. To operate successfully the student team for each firm must organize itself into a decision-making apparatus and then devise and implement various economic strategies as the game moves along, conditions change, and new problems develop.

In the HBS game, students during the course of a semester make dozens of decisions in what is usually 12 decision periods, each of which is defined as a quarter of a "corporate" year. Each student is usually required to spend about 10 hours working out decisions for each period. The staggering number of decisions to make during this time usually induces each member of the firm to become a specialist, such as in marketing, production or some other area. According to McKenney, "firm organization and the resultant specialization are important aspects of the simulation as they generate an organized decision-making group that must solve the firm's internal problems to develop a working team."

As put together by Harvard's gamesters, the simulation represents the economic aspects of making, financing, and selling in an appliance industry that includes toasters, waffle irons and similar goods. Success in the game is determined by how well the performance of the student teams matches the "corporate" goals they set for themselves at the beginning of the game. Like actual companies, the student teams must decide whether their goals will be to increase sales and their share of a mythical market, derive the best possible return on investment, or something else. Such goals, influenced by a fictional history given teams on their companies' past management, must be defended before a "board of directors" made up of Harvard instructors. At the end of the course the instructors grade the students on the realism of the goals they set for themselves and on how well they achieve them. For example, a team whose goal was to improve profitability probably would be graded down if profits remained unimpressive even though sales, for various market reasons, soared upward.

Adding realism to the experience is the fact that the price structure of the goods available for sale in the simulation is similar to the traffic appliance industry where the allowable, feasible product prices range between $4.00 and $44.00.

Also, Harvard's gamesters claim that the production facilities of the model can be considered a generalization of appliance manufacturing operations, since the relationship of capital investment to employees is similar.[5] At the same time, these facilities include a relatively unskilled labor force working in fabrication and assembly departments.

The financial aspects of the modeled firm represent a medium-sized publicly held firm with assets of $4 to $6 million; the firm, according to its "history," has annual normal operating profits of between $400,000 and $600,000. Such a company, according to McKenney, probably would not be financially secure and would require aggressive business plans to survive. All firms in the make-believe industry, then, begin the game very much alike.

But once the game gets underway, "managers" of each firm are free to adopt a wide-ranging set of marketing strategies, such as low price-big volume, or high price-high markup. How well students do implementing such strategies depends on their ability to manipulate what are called the three "demand determinants" of price, product quality and marketing expense. These determinants, says McKenney, "generate an interesting realistic market that allows a rich variety of strategies from nonprice competition to cutthroat pricing."[6]

Allowance also is made in the game for decisions having to do with promotion costs, which can boost demand for a new product or a changed existing product. The game also allows expenses for market research; for example, the purchase of information on potential markets. What happens in the simulated market, then, depends on student decisions governing this range of marketing factors.

While the marketing phase of the game may provide most room for student creativity, decisions also must be made affecting "corporate" production and finance. In the area of production students must deal with what gamesters call a "control problem." That is, they must coordinate inventories, labor and fixed plant and relate decisions in this area to their overall strategy. As the game proceeds students discover, among other things, that there are response lags in the production system to changes in rate or product mix, which result in labor inefficiencies and higher expenses.

In the financial area the student is faced with a "planning problem" requiring the firm to relate internal requirements with a variety of external sources of funds. Creating the internal cash requirement are significant fixed quarterly costs coupled with a highly seasonal market. Students can gain funds by securing loans for their firms if they are able to meet certain financial conditions programmed into the game. Also, each firm has the option of selling its stock at an uncertain price. Harvard gamesters say the stock price relates the total short-run and long-term profit activity of the firm, thus providing the participants with a consistent measure of their own performance. McKenney comments:[7]

"Experience with advanced executives and MBA students has indicated that a challenging gaming experience is developed in an expanding market with limited supply facilities. The challenge is to balance available supply with increasing demand. Thus, in the present model it is relatively easy to expand demand but difficult to take advantage of the expansion and achieve increased profits because of capacity restraints. In part, this approach is due to the nature of the simulations; it is solely an economic representation. In runs where demand has been curtailed and supply is in excess, it has been possible for responsible participant protest to identify forms of noneconomic marketing strategies, such as clever advertising or packaging, which might have allowed a firm to expand. A second reason for the excess demand is that it creates a more exciting game, which seems more fun for the participants as well as the faculty. There are few losers."

How the game works in practice was illustrated recently when 650 first-year graduate students were organized into 21 independent industries as part of large research experiment.[8] Each industry included six or seven five-man firms. The firms competed against each other for three simulated years in an industry modeled by computer to represent a stylized version of the consumer appliance business described above. Each set of decisions, known in game parlance as "a move," represented one quarter of simulated time. Some 76 decisions were made each quarter to determine product quality, marketing effort and production volume, prices and the source and amount of outside financing.

The study was aimed in part at measuring the effects of three different faculty orientations as board members. One group of directors stressed profits, another stressed experimentation in group organization for decision-making and the third stressed activities that would maximize the learning which teams could take from the game into other courses. Each team had a faculty board of directors which encouraged rational play and, at the same time, imparted differing emphases to certain teams.

The boards stressing profits made it clear that they would grade the teams on their success as money-makers.[9] Students were told they would be measured not by the inventiveness of strategies but simply by economic results. Boards stressing experimentation told students they would be graded on how well they functioned as teams, with little or no emphasis on profits. Those boards stressing the game as a vehicle for long-term learning encouraged radical variations in students' play. For these students the game was to be less a competitive economic exercise than a setting in which each man could practice things that would improve his future capabilities as a manager.

What researchers found was a resistance on the part of students to accept different board orientations.[10] Specifically, students tended to resist roles concerned with matters other than profit making. Only one of seven teams encouraged to experiment with various forms of team organization actually did so. Researchers had a bit more success with those teams charged with exploiting "future learning" opportunities provided by games. As a result, Harvard professors were only mildly encouraged that the profit-seeking activity within the game could move students to examine broader business questions outside the game.

What, then, do students learn from such exercises? McKenney declares students do learn things from games as a result of "reflecting on their actions and experiences and from trying to justify their decisions and the resulting economic consequences" to faculty members who serve as boards of directors to the firms. The professor concedes, however, that simulations by themselves are not enough for a complete learning experience. "In act, some of the very things that make such experiences engrossing and exciting may diminish their educational effectiveness," says McKenney.

He adds: "The competitive aspects of a management game, for example, do arouse motivation and help sustain effort. But that may also detract from long-term learning by leading students to play conservative strategies instead of experimenting with new approaches, to emphasize short-term profits within the game context at the expense of building and trying to achieve long-term strategic plans, and to let anxieties about relative performance and grades interfere with efforts to learn." [11]

Some gamesters have attempted to get around such problems by developing even more complex games. One is the Carnegie Tech Management Game, which CIT's Graduate School of Industrial Administration has been developing since

1957. Like the Harvard game, the Carnegie Tech exercise is aimed at providing guided experience in managerial decision-making under conditions of competition and uncertainty. At the same time, the game seeks to advance student skills of analysis, advocacy, and negotiation with outside groups, such as boards of directors and union representatives.

Unlike the Harvard game, which simulates a fictional appliance industry, Carnegie's computer model represents a detergent industry. Reflecting certain real-world features, the model simulates the behavior of consumers in purchasing detergents in retail stores, the behavior of retailers in pricing detergents and ordering them from wholesalers, and the behavior of wholesalers in pricing detergents and ordering them from manufacturers.

Also unlike the Harvard game, whose players make about 76 decisions per move, Carnegie's participants make about 300 per move, or simulated quarter, covering such areas as production, sales, finance, new products, plant facilities and organization. At the end of every simulated year of play, each firm, which consists of from five to 10 players, is required to make a report on its decisions covering these areas to a "board of directors." Managers also must make to the board an evaluation of the present competitive position of the firm; and a review of plans for new investments in products, market development and new plant or warehouse facilities for the future. Students also must explain their reasons for these proposed moves.

The purpose of all these reports, say gamemakers, is to stimulate students to plan their moves thoroughly. In addition to the yearly reports, students also must submit to direcors a set of quarterly plans which they are expected to carry through once they are approved. The game also has been structured to penalize lack of attention to future needs. Indeed, the game is built to dramatize to "executives" the dangers of narrow concentration on one facet of managing a firm. The play of the game forces students to balance specialized and general considerations of a firm.

For example, the Carnegie Tech game lures the careless player into the trap of excessive specialization.[12] The player learns the hard way that the effective manager must learn to be a generalist under conditions where the temptations are strong to remain a specialist. To spur students to consider the firm as a whole, instructors point out to students during the post-game sessions the unsatisfactory income statements and balance sheets of teams that failed to plan and coordinate their activities.

The game also stresses the importance of communication between student "managers" and various business sectors inside and outside the "company." First, students must work together to agree on objectives and means of achieving them. Second, they must work through a subordinate group that implements their policies and decisions. Finally, students must be able to negotiate with their superiors, who may be surrogates of directors, stockholders or others in a position to have an influence on corporate goals and evaluate managerial performance.

In fact, spicing the game is the requirement that each student-businessman, when he sees his firm could use a bank loan, travel into downtown Pittsburgh, a few miles from Carnegie Tech, and actually try to talk a local bank out of some cash, fictional though it may be. There, in the plush chambers of bankers such as Francis S. McMichael, vice president of the Mellon National Bank and Trust Company, the young applicant haggles, bargains and negotiates for the desired amount. Later the student is graded in part on how convincingly he made his case.

As a result of such devices, "students get very absorbed in the competitive aspects of the game," observes Kalman J.

Cohen, professor of economics and industrial administration at Carnegie Tech. "They try harder at games than in some courses." More important, he adds, the exercises "give students an opportunity to practice decision-making techniques or approaches studied in the classroom. They force students to live with the consequences of their decisions, an experience hard to get in the classroom."

As the game proceeds complications are arbitrarily introduced to test players' planning and bargaining abilities. For example, a game administrator may at any time throw into the game an unexpected strike or work slowdown. Players, then, must consider basic personnel questions. Says Cohen: "By introducing more details of a labor market, we could broaden the task to include the questions of wage policy, manpower recruiting and manpower selection."

Carnegie Tech's gamemakers have gone to great lengths to incorporate real-world features into the exercise. Each of the three firms in the mythical detergent industry has a factory which is located in one of four geographical territories that comprise the total detergent market. At this factory are four kinds of facilities: (1) a raw materials warehouse, (2) production facilities that can be used to produce different mixes of product, (3) a factory warehouse for the storage of finished products, and (4) offices and facilities for new product research and development.

In the game each firm markets one or more products which are usually neither very good nor very bad in terms of their basic characteristics: washing power, sudsing power and gentleness. A "company's" sales consist of shipments from its warehouses to the wholesalers or retail chains who are its customers. Firms distribute products at the retail level through supermarkets and grocery stores for home use. As noted earlier, the computer model simulates the behavior of consumers in purchasing detergents in retail stores, the behavior of retailers in pricing detergents and ordering them from manufacturers. Writes Cohen:[13]

"To develop new products or to improve existing products, the teams must spend money for product research and development. Firms can choose to pursue as many as three different kinds of research activities. The most general kind is an unconstrained search for new product ideas. It is also possible to try to synthesize a modification of any product currently being marketed by a competitor or by one's own firm. Finally, management can provide certain specific directions to research effort regarding attributes desired in potential new products. The amount of money spent over time on a research project determines the probability that new product ideas will be generated. The more narrowly a firm defines the goals guiding the expenditure of research funds, the less likely will these funds generate any new product ideas, but the more likely will any new products actually generated satisfy the stipulated goals. As in real life, most new product ideas will not be worth very much; even when a good product is developed, its superiority need not be immediately apparent. Laboratory reports on new products will describe their composition (in terms of the quantities required of up to seven raw materials), the standard labor requirements for them, their characteristics (sudsing power, washing power and gentleness) as revealed by laboratory tests, and the raw material costs per case at standard raw material prices."

In the event players believe a product idea is worth further study, they can spend money to draw a sample of consumers and test their preferences for the characteristics of this new product in comparison with the characteristics of any other product. From "market surveys" such as these, the team will have to decide whether or not to put the product into full-scale production.

The game assumes each company is a "going concern" when players take over its management. At this point the concern already is in business producing and distributing one or more products. Depending on the educational objective of the particular play, the financial conditions in which the firm begins the game can be made to vary. Normally, however, Carnegie Tech's gamemakers start each team in reasonably sound condition with a modest liquid reserve and an established dividend policy.

When financial emergencies develop players can apply for short-term loans from bankers like Mr. McMichaels. To qualify, however, the "company" must meet the same general standards which commercial bankers in reality impose upon firms. Thus, players are informed the bank will consider the history of the firm's deposit balances, its past performances in meeting financial obligations, its overall credit rating, and the reputation of its management. Ultimately the loan is accepted or rejected depending on whether it is prudent or ridiculous when measured against sound banking practices.

As the game proceeds the actions of the players revolve around two basic activities. First, students must analyze the output generated by the computer, and, on the basis of this analysis, they must make decisions. To properly analyze this stream of data, the firms must develop a system of accounting as well as a system for processing the information received. The complexity of the decision-making problems facing students can be better appreciated by looking at the information received in the areas of production, marketing and finance.[14]

Production men, for example, receive forms that summarize information having to do with the raw materials situation, factory performance and warehouse transactions. During the course of the game, they receive at irregular intervals additional facts relating to current hiring and firing costs, current wage rates, price changes and other matters.

As for the marketing man, after each operating period he is informed by the computer about his firm's promotional costs for each product, marketing research expenditures, sales by brand and salesmen's reports on brands introduced by competitors in each region. At various times marketing men also will receive laboratory reports on new products which will scale each of them on sudsing, washing power and gentleness. There will also be reports on raw materials costs and estimates of expected labor productivity in making the new product.

The finance men receive at the end of each month a balance sheet, an income statement, information on the availability of financing and other "facts." They also receive detailed reports on the ways in which accounts are kept and on the ways in which various cash receipts and disbursements occur.

On the basis of such information players running the financial, production and marketing areas of their companies must make a whole complex of decisions. The financial specialists, for example, must decide what share of profits should be allocated as dividends to stockholders and what steps should be taken to cut costs. Production men must decide on the size of the labor force, how much overtime to authorize, how to allocate production among warehouses and a spate of other difficult matters.

Perhaps the area allowing most room for creativity is that of marketing, since it is the decisions made in this area that will determine the concern's sales. The more routine decisions facing marketing men have to do with prices, advertising expenditures and size of sales force. But these players also must deal with a few extremely bizarre questions on which may hinge the success of a team's entire sales effort.

Indeed, one of the most crucial decisions facing marketing men has to do, interestingly, with how "sudsy" to make their detergents. Seemingly frivolous, the question relates to consumer preferences not unlike those in the real world. In some instances players are expected to develop what gamemakers call a "sudsiness" scale covering a range from completely sudsless detergents up to the maximum amount of suds compatible with ordinary usage. The next task is to estimate the distribution of consumer preferences over the various values on the scale.

Student testers in the past have found that the heaviest concentration of usage is centered around a high level of sudsiness, although a substantial proportion of detergent usage also centers around the low end of the scale. Students looking for an explanation of this preference pattern have found that it is largely attributable to the end-use to which the consumer plans to put the particular detergent purchased.

The following insights discovered in the course of playing the Carnegie Tech game are thought to have validity for real-world marketing men:[15]

"In the case of sudsiness, the preferred level is clearly related to the end use of the product. Extensive consumer research has shown that housewives tend to prefer a somewhat sudsy detergent in spite of the fact that suds have little to do with cleaning ability. But to the housewife the presence of suds seems to provide reassurance that the product is doing its job. However, high sudsiness interferes with the operation of automatic washing machines, especially the front-loading type.

"With this information about the major end uses of detergents, we can relate observed preferences to the purpose for which the product is used . . .

"By relating patterns of preferences to the end use of the product, analytically convenient 'submarkets' are defined. A company's own products and those of its competitors can then be evaluated in terms of how well their sudsiness levels fit the pattern of preferences in each such submarket. Changes in the sudsing level of existing products or opportunities for new products can be considered, and possibilities may be seen for improving advertising, promotion, package design and so forth."

In such ways students learn the *realpolitick* of marketing. But the fine calculations of the marketing men, as well as those of the financial and production men, can be rendered almost meaningless by a sudden strike, the possibility for which is determined by the game's administrator. Cohen explains that to give students realistic experience with labor problems, Carnegie Tech's gamemakers have established a collective bargaining agent for the firms' employes called the United Detergent Workers of America (UDWA). The roles of the union representatives are played by faculty members with a special interest in labor, while student teams designate a delegation of their own.

Firms are given copies of the collective bargaining agreement between the UDWA and the company. The agreement sets forth the conditions of employment, expiration date of the contract and procedures that must be used to initiate negotiations for a new contract.

How this aspect of the game works in practice was illustrated in one very elaborate game played a few years ago by Carnegie Tech students and faculty members.[16] Prior to the actual negotiations news releases were issued reporting union elections, and union statements of attitude as the contract termination date approached. During this time union representatives initiated and held meetings with management to discuss certain "pressing problems." Union spokesmen expressed concern for their members, and tried to obtain an agreement from the companies to limit the amount of scheduled overtime.

As a pressure device, Union spokesmen told companies that failure to limit overtime might lead to reductions in productivity and refusal of overtime assignments. Even though protected at this stage by a "no-strike" clause in the agreement, some firms agreed to limit their overtime.

Eventually the union representatives served notice on the firms of their desire to reopen the contract. During the bargaining session the union made demands in several areas. Among other things, the union asked for a wage increase, severance pay and a three-level wage schedule in place of the existing uniform rate. After a great deal of haggling the union did indeed obtain substantial wage increases and improvements in one or more of the other issues.

But not all bargaining sessions end so amicably. One year the three detergent-industry firms, which incidentally negotiate with the union at the same time, succeeded in maintaining a solid front in the labor talks. The result was an industry-wide strike. In another instance, when a different set of student teams were involved, a single firm attempted to obtain a temporary advantage in the industry by giving in quickly to most of the union's demands. This particular company assumed that the other companies would have to give the union at least as much as they had and that, as a result, there might be some gain in a quick settlement.

One company, interestingly, became so involved in the negotiation process that it refused to give in to what it described as the union's "outrageous demands" even after the other two companies had granted them. Consequently this firm found itself in a very serious situation when its plant was struck and the other two companies continued to operate.

Realism is built into this aspect of the game through a number of devices. For one thing, management teams are constrained by their boards and by the impact on their profits of the wage increases and other changes in the labor agreement. Also, artificial constraints are placed on union representatives. In general, the union insisted on the same pattern from all the firms in the industry. In the event one firm was foolish enough to make an unreasonable concession, the union was restrained by the game's rules from forcing others to follow suit. In most cases, however, the union position was that unless a firm could demonstrate a clear possibility of going out of business, it should pay the industry wage.

What do students learn from such confrontations? According to Cohen, the bargaining sessions provided the participants with a dramatic example of the attitudes and values of labor union representatives. He writes:[17]

"There was some surprise and resentment when the union representatives would not accept the company-oriented arguments of the management representatives. The union's emphasis on the short-run, the introduction of institutional variables, and the apparent unwillingness to be concerned about the employment effect of wage increases were sources of conflict in the negotiations. The least profitable firms were particularly enraged at the union's insistence on a uniform pattern. The participants were forced to come to grips with a pattern of behavior they considered irrational. They discovered that the union representatives were unwilling to accept the assumption that management really knows the employes, and they met violent reactions to seemingly innocuous statements which implied that the union did not accurately represent the employes."

The big question, of course, is whether students learn anything from such elaborate exercises that couldn't be learned as well or better through other methods. Few critics of game playing deny that some kind of learning occurs during the course of the exercise. The real question is this: What kind of learning is spurred by games?

Carnegie Tech's gamesters concede there is a need for more studies on what it is precisely students learn as a result of playing games. Nevertheless, they claim there are observable changes in students who participate in the exercises. According to Cohen, they become quicker and more sophisticated about abstracting, organizing and using information from a complex and diffuse environment. Also, they become better at distinguishing between valuable and trivial information, and, finally, they become more effective at coordinating information and actions between the separate functions of marketing, production and finance.

What some scholars hope students derive from games is the ability to be "general and structural" rather than bound to specialized content or issues.[18] At the same time, some gamemakers worry that what is learned pertains largely if not wholly to playing the game more effectively.

To avoid this pitfall, Carnegie Tech, Harvard and some other schools place a great deal of stress on the post-game evaluation sessions in which students meet with their instructors and other faculty members who had roles in the game. In these sessions students are required to generalize from their experiences about the broader management questions raised by the game. Also, they receive the game's "payoff." That is, they learn how well they performed in terms of their own objectives established prior to actual play; they are, in effect, measured against their own yardsticks. How well a first year graduate student plays the game may account for as much as half of his grade in a Carnegie Tech or Harvard business policy course.

Students themselves are enthusiastic about the exercises. From a number of post-game interviews, researchers have found that the primary "sources of learning" for players were in the personal relationships formed during the course of the game. Cohen observes that "students remember what they learn from interactions with other people more vividly than they remember what they learned from working on the competitive tasks in the game." [19]

In one interview most student comments pertained to organizational learning. "We had to be able to justify things (to the board) as well as to get them done," one student told a Carnegie Tech instructor. Another added: "I have learned to look for influence patterns and have learned about their importance in a way which I don't think I would have done just from the courses only." Students were much less inclined to cite experiences with the computer model as a source of learning.

Whether or not it is an effective learning aid, the game and various versions of it have spread to a spate of business schools. Games similar to the Carnegie Tech model have been played at Tulane University, the University of Pittsburgh, the University of North Carolina, Indiana University and the University of Oklahoma.

However, by no means do all business games model only domestic companies or industries. One of the most interestin business games developed is the International Operations Simulation (INTOP) used by the University of Chicago's Graduate School of Business. INTOP is the first major business simulation exercise oriented toward the specific problems of international trade and overseas operations. Developed in the early 1960's, Chicago's gamesters say the exercise "derives special significance from the fact that international operations—and competition from abroad in domestic markets—will become an increasingly vital element in the evolving enterprise system of the 1960's." [20]

Like the Harvard and Carnegie Tech games, INTOP requires a computer, which, according to Chicago gamemakers, "allows for the feeding-in of as many judgmental factors, acts of God and changes in the overall environment as it pleases any individual administrator to introduce."[21] INTOP provides for three to 15 company teams, each consisting of four to seven student executives.

Chicago gamemakers bill the exercise as one that forces participants into a stream of top management decisions of business philosophy and objectives, as opposed "to the heavy strategy-tactics emphasis" of most other games. This is accomplished, they say, by continually facing the teams with the choice of representing national or international companies, and the need to decide what business activities they will undertake.

In the game, the companies operate in one, two or all of three *areas*—Brazil, the European Economic Community (EEC), or the United States. By "operate" Chicago researchers mean a business activity that may cover any one or any combination, of the functions of manufacturing, marketing of one's product, serving as a distributor and licensing. It is even possible for a company to restrict itself to the role of financier and/or research institution. If an INTOP company so chooses, it can view itself as a corner appliance in Rio while another aspires to be Global Electric. However, all concerns are assumed to have their home office in the country of Liechtenstein, which is described as a "well-known international tax haven."

The first action of each company team is to set down in written form its general business philosophy and operating objectives along with strategies to implement them. The imaginativeness of this planning effort in itself provides one criterion of performance, which, as in other business games, is determined in post-game evaluation sessions.

As in real life, each of the three areas has its peculiar characteristics in terms of size, demand and production functions. Also, each area is peculiar in terms of economic climate and governmental policies with regard to corporate taxation and international trade. The game's administrator programs into the game acts of God and other difficulties that may afflict the companies from time to time. For example, countries with balance-of-payments troubles may place restrictions on the remittance of profits abroad.

There are transfer costs—representing transportation, insurance, customs, paperwork, etc.—between the areas. As the game proceeds these charges may be varied as nations revise tariff rates or as costs of shipping fluctuate. Nations may impose import quotas to stimulate local manufacturing, to reduce the sales of luxury products, or as an anti-dumping measure—matters, incidentally, usually determined by the administrator.

Each company may manufacture and/or market either or both of two different products, which are usually two medium-priced electrical appliances. The game, however, doesn't purport to "reproduce" any one specific real-life market in detail, since the purpose of the exercise is to tackle business problems in general.

Companies may improve their products through research and development. The game's rules allow each of the two products to have up to four improvements (or "grades") during the play. Realism is carried to a fine degree, since patents may be licensed, globally or nationally, selectively or exclusively, and with provision as to the maintenance of minimum prices. The complexity of the game's play is described by its designers:[22]

"Due to the plurality of products, grades and geographical markets with different demand characteristics, marketing management decisions are crucial. In the end consumer markets price elasticity varies with all three of these categories, while advertising extends to both grades of a given product which a company may sell in a given consumer market at any given time. The consumer market in any given area may be approached by three channels: by using other companies as distributors, by manufacturer's agents, or by a captive sales organization. In general, these channels are all equally effective in reaching the market; hence the channel problem is essentially one of minimizing cost at the estimated sales volumes and rates of growth. The channels employed may be national or international, and the company may also transfer its own goods from one area to another [intra-company transactions] . . .

"Marketing research is encouraged by the provision of a wealth of market and company operating data each quarter. Companies may decide to pay for an array of additional market studies available on a contract basis."

The game is given a strong flavor of international finance by the fact that interest rates as well as corporate tax rates and carry-forward rules vary among the three areas and Liechtenstein. Also, governments may place restrictions—or incentives—on capital transfers. In cases of financial difficulty, suppliers may be counted on to extend emergency aid, but only on stiff terms. When the patience of suppliers and the game's simulated bankers is exhausted, the company involved is forced into bankruptcy or merger.

To place a premium on planning, gamemakers have added other dynamic features to the game. For example, there are time lags of one or several quarters in plant construction, international transfers of goods, use of patents, maturing of accounts receivable and payable, the international spread of business cycle effects.

Here are a sampling of decisions made by one "company" which decided to enter the portable transistor radio business on an international scale. In both the United States and the EEC the firm was a producer-marketer of radios, while in

Brazil it marketed radios imported from its American and European factories. According to a data report for its 12th quarter, the firm imported 10,000 standard, or low-cost, units from the United States, while an equal number of deluxe, or high-cost, units came in from Europe, ready for sale to Brazilians in quarter 13.

To the game's administrators this arranemegnt seemed sensible, even though the shipment from the United States probably lessened the company's standard sales there. As Chicago gamesters explain it, greater standard sales would have eaten into the company's deluxe sales in the United States. According to researchers, shipping deluxe units from the EEC was wise since the company was still left with what, for the local deluxe radio market, was fairly hefty inventory.[23]

The Chicago game raises the same questions about learning effects as do other business games. Chicago's gamemakers claim the exercise is meaningful because it is able to effectively pose classical management dilemmas. For example, researchers note that while players would like to be everything to everybody, success is linked to specialization and differential advantage. Thus, teams doing best by conventional economic criteria are those which supplement their own narrow base of specialization with mutually advantageous cooperative arrangements with other companies in the game.

Nor is this all; researchers claim the behavior of players jibes with real-life observation of business behavior. For example, players have a tendency to be oversensitive to relatively modest changes in the general business climate, while they tend to be relatively insensitive to long-run structural changes whose aggregate impact on the simulated economies is much larger. This is also a failing of executives in real-life, say educators.

Chicago's gamemakers concede that what is actually learned from the experience is often too intangible to measure precisely. However, they note that INTOP's participants claim the experience increases their awareness of the interrelatedness of various parts of a business. There is no question such games spur tremendous involvement, which, at least in part, must be attributed to the fact that one-half of the course grade may depend on a student's performance in the exercise.

Games are useful because "they force students to live with the consequences of their decisions; this type of 'learning from experience' is very hard to get in the normal course," says Kalman Cohen. But he reminds that "a simulation game doesn't constitute a total educational program." They should be viewed, he contends, as part of a larger educational effort in which lectures, case studies and other conventional teaching techniques are brought into play. This being said, Cohen insists that games "give students opportunities to practice techniques studied in the classrooms." At the same time, he adds: "They also provide learning not directly related to quantitative decision-making. Students learn about organizational behavior; they often acquire insights into interpersonal relationships with other team members."

For the most part, business games emphasize the quantitative factors involved in decision-making. Political games, however, often go to greater lengths to deal with qualitative—or human—factors in decision making. As will be seen, programming such factors into political simulations requires a fundamentally different approach to model building.

Chapter 3

POLITICAL GAMES: SACRED AND PROFANE

"War is a statesman's game, a priest's delight . . ."—***Shelley***

At Northwestern's Department of Political Science, 25 students enter a large laboratory and take seats around five tables separated by partitions. Couriers scurry back and forth, carrying messages between the enclosed tables and occasionally dropping them off at a smaller table in the center of the room. The table bears the sign, "World Newspaper." Off to one side is a calculation table, where game administrators plot the effects of moves initiated by the decision-makers. Some of the moves are transcribed onto punch cards and taken to a computer programmed with certain cause-and-effect formulas.

Meantime, a good 2,000 miles away at the San Francisco Theological Seminary at San Anselmo, Calif., a similar number of students file into a somewhat ramshackle room and also group themselves around a set of tables. They immediately plunge into background reading on various non-existent churches, such as Bigdome Presbyterian Church or Gotrocks Presbyterian Church, all located in make-believe Augustine City. In both cases, the students are playing two very different but related political games; the games are political because both deal with how institutions can be understood and, in some bases, manipulated in the larger social arena.

The San Anselmo students, in training for the Presbyterian ministry, are playing "Augustine City," a recently developed game adapted for use in a course entitled *Pastoral Leadership in the Local Church.* The game is aimed at representing the various pressures which the pastor meets in his job.[1] The Northwestern students are playing Inter-Nation Simulation (INS), a simplified operating model of the international system, which is being used to supplement courses in international relations at a number of universities.

Taken together the two games represent the growing emphasis on what some educators call "learning through vicarious decision-making." The idea is at least as old as William James, who in 1892 exhorted teachers to make learning more activity-oriented. "*No reception without reaction, no impression without expression*," James told teachers in a famous essay. "Laboratory work and shop work," he went on to say, "engender a habit of observation, a knowledge of the difference between accuracy and vagueness, and an insight into nature's complexity and into the inadequacy of all abstract verbal accounts of real phenomena. . . ."[2]

More recently, Johns Hopkins' James Coleman has contended that students need an opportunity to *act* on what they are taught, to "take the role of the other." And Jerome Bruner, an educator whose theories have spurred educational gaming trends, has argued that provision for vicarious experience is a necessary adjunct to other modes of learning.[3]

The wisdom of such notions seem borne out by those psychologists who assert, contrary to some of the country's deepest Puritan beliefs, that pleasure in the laboratory task brings important reinforcement to learning.[4] At Northwestern, Richard Snyder, co-director of the school's International Relations Program, calls INS "a most effective means of bringing distant policy realism within the individual's personal experience in a manner which cannot be matched by other teaching materials."

INS was devised in 1958 by a research team headed by Northwestern's Harold Guetzkow, who, with Snyder, directs the university's International Relations Program. Developed originally under the auspices of the Carnegie Corp. and the Air Force, the simulation at present is being used at Northwestern for research purposes on a $90,000 Defense Department grant. At the same time, it is used by undergraduates studying international relations. In addition to its use by a number of universities, the game has been revised and simplified for use in secondary schools. Currently, the game is being marketed commercially—at $55 per game—by Science Research Associates, Inc., a Chicago-based subsidiary of IBM Corp. Right now non-computer versions of INS are being used in about 200 high schools.

Like the Carnegie Tech and Harvard business exercises, the Northwestern version of INS is a man-machine game. As such, the simulation must be distinguished from those political games that are either "all-manual" or "all-computer." All-manual exercises involve human participants without using computers to determine the effects of players' actions on the game situation. Some—though by no means all—of these exercises are reminiscent of the centuries-old "free" war games in which the only restrictions on the actions of decision-makers are prescribed by scenarios and other men—the umpires. Such umpires are generally "free" to calculate the impact of moves on the basis of subjective judgment.

Even though manual, "free" games nevertheless are often quite complex. An example is the crisis exercise developed by the Rand Corp. in the early 1950's which involved the creation of a "scenario," embodying some particular real-world policy problem.[5] These scenarios were then handed out to players assembled into "nations." The teams, or nations, then "played out" the crisis situation, their moves being monitored by an umpire or "control" team just as in a war game. Similar games are now being developed at the Massachusetts Institute of Technology, the Foreign Policy Research Institute at the University of Pennsylvania, and by Herman

Kahn and his associates at the Hudson Institute.

However, manual games are not necessarily always "free." Some are "rigid," just as some early war games were rigid in that the effects of moves taken by decision-makers were determined by an elaborate rule book. A modern example is Dangerous Parallel, developed recently by the Foreign Policy Association for use in high schools. In Dangerous Parallel, which will be discussed fully in the next chapter, the outcomes of moves made by players are determined by a rule book prepared in advance of the game.

All-computer games—in which there are no human players—are necessarily "rigid." An example is TEMPER, developed by the Raytheon Co. in 1964. The Joint War Games Agency of the Office of the Joint Chiefs of Staff commissioned the firm to build an extensive and complex digital computer simulation, which is called a Technological, Economic, Military and Political Evaluation Routine (thus the name, TEMPER).

In TEMPER and other all-computer simulations, a model of decision-making behavior is included as part of the larger model to replace the human decision-makers found in man-machine games.[6] The advantage of this approach, apparently, is that it offers a quick and inexpensive way of playing out several different strategies for desired periods of future time.

As a man-machine game, Northwestern's INS is an attempt to combine the advantages of both all-computer and all-manual exercises. According to Guetzkow, the game involves a mix of men and machines and "free" and "rigid" elements. The simulation is rigid in that some of its variables are programmed in their relationships, meaning the exercise requires a computer to calculate the impact of some moves. These moves largely have to do with internal development—political and economic—of a fictional nation. But the game also allows for a good deal of "free activity," actions and counteractions between nations in which the consequences are not programmed in advance.

What, then, is an inter-nation simulation? The Northwestern game is an attempt to represent nations in their interrelations with each other. To make the exercise manageable, game-makers have reduced and simplified the number of variables actually involved in such relations. As defined by Guetzkow, INS is an "operating representation in reduced and/or simplified form of relations among social units by means of symbolic and/or replicate component parts." [7]

Put a little more simply, INS is based on a model, which is a collection of assertions about some reality—past, present or predicted.[8] In effect, a model is a set of statements which purports to describe relationships holding between component parts of that reality. Thus, to build a model, the game-maker, or theorist, must abstract from reality those components and relationships that are considered crucial to what is being modeled. In the end, model-builders hope their creations resemble the reality they represent. Whether they do is determined through elaborate experiments involving the games.

In this way, researchers hope in time simulations will aid them in making predictions about international political developments. While there are similarities, political games such as INS differ importantly from business games, which reside on somewhat different propositions. The models that underpin business simulations are based on classical game theory developed by von Neumann anad Morgenstern. Operating models called political games are quite distinct entities. As one Northwestern scholar puts it: [9]

"The theory of games ('game theory') provides a means of describing the strategic behavior of one or more actors who have to make choices in conflict situations (games) in which the payoffs (potential outcomes) are a function of the choices made by all parties to the conflict. The Game Theory model is normative, in that it prescribes the choice or combination of choices which lead to the *best* payoff under the circumstances of a given conflict situation. The theory, moreover, postulates a 'rational' actor who will always follow the best strategy. A political game (or simulation) is an operating model which represents an attempt on the part of the theorist, through the representation of an empirical system, to provide himself with information about states of the real system."

Consequently, Inter-Nation Simulation has been widely used as a research tool. Charles and Margaret Hermann of Princeton University have used INS with data from World War I to determine the validity of the model, even going so far as to match the personality traits of the actors with the leaders of 1914. Researchers at Yale have used simulation to investigate responses to a hypothetical nuclear attack from an unknown source.

Some of the most ambitious research has been done at Northwestern, which used INS to study the long-run effects of the proliferation of nuclear weapons on alliances. The experimental design placed some nine nations in the INS, organized initially in two bloc alliances. Researchers recall that 15 replications of the simulation were each allowed to run for six simulated "years," with only the largest nation of each bloc having a nuclear force capability. Then nuclear capabilities were gained gradually by all the other nations.

Purpose of the research was to determine whether alliances remained cohesive despite spreading nuclear capabilities. "The central finding," says Guetzkow, "was that alliances tended to become fragmented, a long-run prediction that is looking more and more valid as one watches nuclear-weapons capabilities spread throughout the world of the 1960's." [10]

An increasingly important use of games is to teach the participant, rather than simply inform the researcher. Among the claimed benefits of simulations, the chief one is that the exercises heighten the interest and motivation of the students in several ways. For one thing, the activity of most simulations appears to be more enjoyable than conventional kinds of learning, according to Northwestern's Chadwick Alger.[11]

Also, he claims games stimulate students to learn because of the immediate application they can make of knowledge acquired in the classroom. Finally, he says games provide students with a mutually shared experience which stimulates discussion with fellow-students outside of class far more than normal course work.

But Northwestern educators claim the simulations do more than simply motivate the players. According to Alger, games also offer insights into aspects of the decision-maker's predicament that are assumed to be peculiar to the institutions being simulated. Some Rand gamesters have alleged that players acquire "new insights into the pressures, the uncertainties, and the moral and intellectual difficulties under which foreign policy decisions are made."[12] Further, games are said to provide a miniature world that is easier for the player to comprehend as a whole than the real institutions themselves.

Simulations may be much simpler than the reality they represent. At the same time, they are often exceedingly complex, which is amply demonstrated by the actual workings of INS. The simulation involves five "nation" units, each of which consists of three or more participants—a "central decision-maker" holding office, one or two "external decision-makers," and an "aspiring decision-maker," who is out of office. The development of relations among these nations is an outgrowth of their leaders' ambitions and their differing levels of political and economic development.

In the laboratory, the participants are physically proximate, but only written communications are permitted. This allows researchers to obtain a complete record of transactions between players. Within a nation, the CDM and the EDM pass messages back and forth by sliding them through a barrier separating the two halves of the table at which they are seated. As noted earlier, the tables themselves are separated by screens.

Nonparticipating messengers carry notes from one EDM to another. Carbons of all messages are given to a researcher-reporter, so that reports for the newspaper can be prepared from those not marked "RESTRICTED." A larger room nearby is used for international conferences. Other rooms are set aside for possible sessions of an international organization, which may be formed in the process of playing the game. In addition, a lounge is provided for informal contact among persons assigned by their nations to the international organization.

An hour is usually allowed for each period of the simulation. Half-way through the period, the CDMs complete decision forms on moves decided upon. Decision forms in hand, researchers use them to calculate the probabilities of the CDM remaining in office, which, not surprisingly, is one of the CDM's central concerns in the game. The consequences of decisions made by each "nation" are returned to decision-makers at the beginning of the following period.

As explained by Guetzkow, the researchers, in calculating outcomes, use a combination of rigid rules and subjectives judgments. For example, the strength of states is mechanically determined from their strategic strength allocations, as combined through their alliances.

At the same time, subjective judgments are made by the simulation director as to how well a nation is achieving its particular goals, which vary from nation to nation and are usually set at the outset of the game. Goals, which range from security, domination, cooperation to internal growth, depend on a nation's mythical "history" and "strength."

Here is how one Northwestern gamester describes the simulation's workings:[13]

"The internal organization of the nation is determined in large measure by the participants. The central decision-maker represents the chief of state and performs the executive function of government. He maintains his position by satisfying those who validate his office-holding. The external decision-makers represent the foreign relations structure of the nation and perform the corresponding function. They are dependent upon the central decision-maker for continuance in office . . . The apportionment of responsibilities among the decision-makers is optional. The aspiring decision-maker(s) represent leaders of competing elites in the nation who seek to gain office.

"The more highly programmed part of the simulation is the set of relations among the intranational factors. . . . Each nation contains a set of decision-makers. They maintain themselves in office by virtue of their ability to satisfy intranational groups who validate their office-holding. Satisfactions are derived by these 'validators' from two sources, each intended to represent a cluster of factors operating in the political, economic and social life of the nation. Given the basic capability of his simulated nation, the central decision-maker periodically makes short-term allocations to: (1) the validators' consumption of goods and services; and/or (2) his nation's force capability, both of which yield satisfactions for the validating groups. It is also possible for the central decision-maker to plan for the long-term by allocating his nation's basic resources to the generation of more basic capability, which in turn may be used for future allocations. The opposing aspirant decision-maker appears to the same validators in the hope of getting into office."

Who are these validators? They exist in the game only conceptually; their function is represented by certain decision consequences computed by the researcher. They have wants and goals that are more or less satisfied by governmental decisions. If they are satisfied, they will tend to support the CDM's tenure in office. If dissatisfied, however, they will support the efforts of the aspiring decision-maker to acquire office.

As in real life, however, there exist complications that may thwart the validators from translating their dissatisfaction into opposition to the CDM. This ability of validators to express opposition varies from nation to nation; the effectiveness of validator support or opposition is expressed as "decision-latitude." The concept expresses the sensitivity of the relation of decision-makers to validators. On the one hand, a CDM in a dictatorial system allowing a great amount of decision latitude may operate with relative impunity. Even though heedless of his validators, his likelihood of retaining power is not dependent on their satisfaction or dissatisfaction.

But INS also includes nations whose political systems resemble those of democracies. In these cases the CDM must ponder seriously the dissatisfaction of his validators, for his ability to retain office depends to a great extent on the satisfaction of his validators. In all cases, however, a central decision-maker may lose office, either through orderly procedures or a revolution.

But nations do not remain isolated while their central decision-makers are balancing these internal pressures. Interrelations among the nations may develop in any number of ways. According to game-makers, some of the nations may trade their resources, either in "raw" form as basic capability, or in converted form as force capability and consumption "units." Some nations may make grants of aid to other nations within the system. Alliances may be formed, based upon inter-nation treaties. Nations may establish international organizations. Should conflict develop, nations may even go to war against each other.

Nations begin play with varying "capabilities" that fall into to two main categories—"basic" and "force" capabilities.[14] Basic capability represents all kinds of a nation's basic resources, physical and human. According to the INS player's manual, the size of a nation's basic capability accumulation reflects the nation's over-all, fundamental ability to produce all other goods and services. Thus, it provides a changing measure of national wealth. Says the INS manual:

"Decisions are made each period by the central decision-maker as to the kinds of production to which his nation's basic capability accumulation will be allocated. Each nation is given an initial amount of basic capability units (BC's) at the beginning of the simulation. These are available for allocation during the first period. Additions to the nation's BC accumulation may be achieved by: (1) devoting some portion of the initial amount to the generation of *new* BC's, or (2) the receipt of BC's from other nations in trade or aid."

Researchers point out that validator satisfaction *is not* directly related to the amount of BC's a nation possesses. Instead, its relationship is indirect through growth in the nation's ability to generate goods *which are* directly related to validator satisfaction.

During game periods, decision-makers may devote a portion of a nation's basic capability to the production of goods and services to support the population. In INS parlance, these items are called "consumption satisfaction" units (CS's). They represent all goods and services which contribute to the standard of living of the population, particularly the validator's.

In each period of play, the CDM *must* allow a specified minimum number of CS's to remain in the nation for consumption. The chief-of-state does this by allocating a portion of his basic capability to the generation of CS units, or by receipt of so-called CS's from other nations in trade or aid. Validator satisfaction with regard to consumption is calculated by the researcher after decision forms are collected for each period of play. It is determined by the ratio of the number of CS's actually left in the nation to a minimum consumption standard set by researchers. As the INS manual makes clear, this is no simple matter:

"The relationship between the validator satisfaction with regard to consumption satisfaction and the above ratio may vary among the several nations and at different times. This represents variation in the intensity of validator wants. Generally, the greater the number of CS's actually remaining in the nation compared to the minimum consumption standard, the greater the validator satisfaction. This relationship is not the same for all nations; the validators in nations having significantly greater capacity for generating CS's are less sensitive to given changes in the number of CS's received than are the validators with little capacity to produce CS's."

Also, at the beginning of the game each nation is given a certain number of force capability units, called FC units by gamesters. Again, the CDM has the option of adding to this amount through foreign aid from another nation or by devoting some portion of his initial basic capability to the generation of FC's. Once again, validator satisfaction with regard to national security is calculated by the game administrator after decision forms are collected after each period. Such satisfaction is determined by another ratio measure, this one representing the strength of a nation and its allies in relation to the strongest nation (or group of nations) not allied with it. This strength measure includes both force capability and basic capability, the latter of which is regarded as potential force capability.

In most cases, validator satisfaction is related to the relative strategic position of a nation—although only to a certain point. In fact, beyond a certain point validator satisfaction ceases to increase with increases in a nation's relative strategic position. This is because game-makers hypothesize there is a "maximum point" beyond which validators become indifferent to such increases.

During the simulation, players find there are two uses to which force capability may be put—war and internal controls in the nation. As the game is structured, participants during play find it is prudent to allocate at least part of their force capability to internal control, although the size of such allocations will depend on many considerations. But according to the game's cause-and-effect relationships, the *probability of successful* revolution, should revolution occur, depends upon the degree of internal control the CDM exercises over the validators in nation.

Northwestern gamesters explain that the game is programmed in such a way that without the application of internal controls revolutionary potential builds, particularly in the more or less "authoritarian" systems in which the CDM's decision latitude is increasing. Absence of such controls, then, increases the possibility of a coup d'etat or revolt, either of which may occur when validator satisfaction falls below a certain point determined by the computer's cause-and-effect formulas. Thus, internal controls are an important political tool for the CDM.

But when internal political pressures build up, decision-makers remain free to opt for reduction of such pressures through international adventures. These may lead to war or elaborate peace conferences. When war does occur, however, the belligerent nations receive an automatic two-unit increase in over-all validator satisfaction for the period of play in the hostilities break out. The problem for the central decision-maker is that this "rallying to the cause" effect does not last.

Indeed, for each decision period the war lingers on, validator satisfaction decreases by one unit.

When one nation declares war on another, the "attacking nation" must indicate on a decision form the amount of force capability it is committing to the war. In so doing, it may allocate all or any part of its total FC's which are not currently in use for internal controls. If the attacking nation's allies go to war simultaneously, they also must indicate force capability commitments.

The "target nation," the nation against which war has been declared, has 15 minutes to respond to the declaration. This allows time for consultation with allies, although the nation may respond with or without allies in any way it sees fit. If the target nation declares war in return, it also must indicate the amount of force capability being committed to the conflict. If the target nation decides to take no action, the outcome of the war is decided solely by the attacking nations.

But if both sides declare war, the game administrator then announces publicly the probability of victory for each side. After this announcement a 15-minute period is allowed for communication between the belligerents. At the end of this period the situation is again assessed. As the INS manual explains, only three states of affairs are possible: [15]

1. The two sides may have negotiated a peace settlement.

2. The two sides may have agreed to call for a decision on the outcome of the war on the basis of the probabilities of victory or defeat announced earlier by the administrator. This simulates a "decisive battle," and, being such, *both sides must agree to it.*

3. If agreement cannot be reached on numbers 1 or 2, both sides will be called upon for new commitments of force capability to a continuing war. These new commitments are mandatory; 15 minutes are allowed for the respective sides to consult and decide upon the size of the new commitments.

Then, the procedure is repeated until either number 1 or number 2 is the outcome of the negotiations.

The war is not without costs. At the end of each negotiating period between belligerents, the force capability commitments made at the outbreak of hostilities are considered consumed by the war. In addition to the war's economic and military costs, there are other consequences. In case 1 the additional consequences depend upon the peace settlement that is negotiated. Case 3 prolongs the war and postpones these additional consequences. In case 2—a call for a "decisive battle"—the nation losing the battle is considered to have surrendered unconditionally and to have been occupied. How occupation works is described by Northwestern's Professor Noel:[16]

"The decision-makers of the occupied nations are forced into 'exile.' They may continue to communicate among themselves and with other nations as usual, and they may work to organize support for a liberation movement. However, they remain 'stateless persons' until they are able to liberate their country or until they are invited by the conqueror to return to office. The decision form of the occupied nation is given, along with full power of decision, to the CDM of the victorious nation. He operates in the occupied nation with maximum latitude, and can only be dislodged from power by a successful war of liberation or a successful revolution; there are no regular office holding determinations. Revolution, that is, attempts to overthrow the conqueror, may still happen in the usual way. In fact, they are highly probable. Each period of occupation may trigger one, because the presence of unwanted 'foreigners' in the country creates dissatisfaction—amounting to one-unit decrease per period in over-all dissatisfaction—among the ever-present validators . . .

"Also, the occupying CDM operates with such high decision

latitude as to inflate the probability of having a revolution. However, he may reduce the risk of revolution and, at the same time, assure one little chance of success by applying *his own* FC's to internal controls within the occupied nation. Any FC's belonging to the conquered nation cannot be relied upon for occupation use. . . .

"Barring a successful liberation or revolution, the length of the occupation is determined by the occupier. He may withdraw his forces at any time, or he may continue the occupation indefinitely. Should he withdraw, he may establish a new government to his liking. He may negotiate with the deposed CDM or with the aspiring CDM to do so; or he may request (the administrator) that other 'nationals' of the occupied nation be established as decision-makers . . ."

How involved the game can get was illustrated when some 30 Northwestern students in the social sciences participated in 16 three-hour sessions. The students divided themselves into five mythical lands with varying "histories" and "capabilities." They were Omne and Utro—two relatively strong nations with high productivity rates—and Algo, Erga and Engo—three weak nations with limited economic potential. It wasn't long before the nations found themselves snared in a maelstrom of international tensions. For one thing, both Omne and Utro, through various machinations, grew richer while the economies of the other countries faltered and sputtered. Fueling the uneasiness was the growing military strength of Omne, which alarmed even Utro.

The foreign policy chief, or external decision-maker, of Erga responded to the situation by calling an international conference. The Erga policy-maker let it be known that, in his view, the economic plight of the small nations, as well as the threat posed by Omne, could be solved if all the nations could just get around a conference table and talk things over.[17]

At the conference this decision-maker advocated establishment of an international bank through which the wealthy countries would aid the poorer ones. Squabbling developed, however, when the wealthy nations resisted the idea. Although all nations voted for a resolution supporting in principle establishment of such a bank, it was never created. The wealthy nations did offer to extend some aid to the poorer ones, but on a bilateral rather than a multilateral basis.

The nations also failed to agree on a strategy to check Omne. Soon Utro started an arms program of its own. Eventually two blocs developed as a result of secret alliances: Omne-Ingo and Utro-Erga. Through such means the two big powers hoped to avoid the dangers of finding themselves isolated in a hostile "world." The small nations had two objectives: military security plus a vehicle to economic favors.

The only nation left out of the alliance system was Algo, the poorest nation of all. During a bilateral conference, Omne suggested to the somewhat impoverished Ingo that Algo be requested to join their alliance. Fearful that Algo might siphon off some of the economic aid it was receiving from Omne, Ingo suppressed the idea by casting suspicion on Algo's dependability as an ally.

Not surprisingly, Algo's decision-makers became increasingly worried about their military vulnerability and their ebbing economic fortunes. After considerable internal wrangling, Algo's policy-makers concluded that only a radical change in the world system of power could save them. Consequently, they devised a plan to incite such a realignment.

What Algo did was fabricate a message from Erga to its ally Utro in which it was indicated the two countries planned to attack Ingo. Algo arranged it for the message to fall surreptitiously into the hands of Ingo's decision-makers. Believing itself the target for a pending "attack," Ingo called an international conference to reveal the plot to the world.

At an emotion-filled conference Erga denied authorship of the note. Algo offered to mediate the dispute between the two blocs, but when tempers flared and tension mounted Algo was forced to admit its authorship of the note. At first Algo insisted the ruse was necessary to spur a conference that would save the world form its declining state of affairs. But later an Algo leader admitted: "We hoped that Algo could gain its rightful place in world affairs through offering its services as mediator; or should this prove unacceptable, it would remain at peace and emerge from the conflict ahead of the war-torn countries."

Despite its brinkmanship, Algo nevertheless obtained a secret military pact and economic aid from Omne. Omne decided to keep the pact secret and use Algo as a potential neutral listening post for information on its strongest enemy, Utro.

Not all games end so happily, however. Indeed, a few have ended in nuclear conflagration. How this can happen was illustrated in another play of INS by Northwestern undergraduates in which Omne and Utro were again the dominant powers. However, Utro suffered a revolution when it failed to allocate sufficient resources to consumer goods while concentrating on the arms race with Omne. These internal troubles left Utro a second-class power, far behind Omne in arms development.

Meantime, an international meeting was called, and, after a long period of hard bargaining, the two nuclear powers, Omne and Utro, agreed to turn their nuclear weapons over to a newly-formed world body. All nations agreed to turn two-thirds of their conventional weaponry over to the world organization. Much of the initiative for these moves came from Omne. But because of Omne's economic and military superiority, the other nations remained suspicious of her intentions.

At the same time, Utro balked at its number two status in the world arena. In private sessions, Utro's policy-makers made it known to each other that the prospect of remaining perpetually number two was unattractive. One might say they decided to "try harder." Thus, they set about framing a strategy aimed at improving their strategic position.

As a result of lingering suspicions the terms of the disarmament agreement were never implemented. During this period of confusion over disarmament, Utro moved to regain its former position of international dominance. The country hastily allocated all available resources into nuclear weapons, a development that went undetected by the other nations. After establishing nuclear superiority over Omne, Utro presented the surprised Omnians with an ultimatum.

In effect, Utro demanded that Omne either surrender its sovereignty to Utro or face destruction. Desperate, Omne's leaders sought to gain time through lengthy negotiations, but Utro's patience soon ran out. The result: Utro attacked and reduced Omne to the level of the three minor powers.

Utro then sought to build a world order its leaders predicted would be "just and profitable" for all. But by this time Utro had lost the trust of the smaller nations. While Utro was concentrating on developing the new Utro-Omne economy, the other nations federated and used their combined resources to develop nuclear weapons. With Utro preoccupied the three small nations launched a pre-emptive attack on it—which left the one-time nuclear giant in ruins. Before the shooting ended, however, Utro had time to devastate Erga, leaving only two nations relatively unscathed. The game ended with distrust and suspicion permeating the relations among the surviving nations.

What do students learn from such grisly exercises? According to Professor Alger, who conducted the game, students cite six kinds of learning produced by the game experience.

Basing his conclusions on student responses to a questionnaire, Alger suggests the game does the following:[18]

1. Provides vividness and understanding beyond what one gets from a textbook.
2. Gives one a realization of the complexities of conflicts between rival nations.
3. Indicates the importance of having reliable knowledge and the importance of communication in international relations.
4. Develops better understanding of the problems and goals of nations not like the United States.
5. Enables participants to better understand the problems of decision-making.
6. Demonstrates the difficulties of balancing the requirements of internal and external affairs.

Some benifits cf p. 9

There is no question about student enthusiasm. After the session, some said they had increased empathy for the plight of small nations in the world arena, while others felt they better understood the phenomenon of nationalism. "I feel like an Omnian," one student confided to an instructor. "In other words, I have developed a nationalist patriotism, pride in Omne's achievements and distress over its failures, which in many ways is just as strong as my American patriotism."

Said another: "The awareness of the vast number and the complexity of the factors which must be considered by a nation could never have been as vivid from reading a book."

Finally, one student said: "Another important thing I now understand better is communism. I realized to my amazement when we made out the decision sheet for Ingo that even those of us who claimed to be staunch conservatives were advocating pushing economic development as hard as we could, disregarding as far as we dared the validators. Our 'motto' was to bring the people as close as possible to starvation without there being a revolution. Now I can see why communism has such appeal among the underprivileged nations of the world. The temptation to move swiftly ahead at all costs is a strong one indeed, and this is especially true if you have nothing to conserve (thus why be a conservative?)."

INS is one of a wide variety of political simulations currently being played by college students. One used recently at New York University in a course on "The United Nations at Work" involves students simulating the main councils and committees of the United Nations. International relations simulations are currently being used at the Air Force Academy, the Massachusetts Institute of Technology, the University of Wisconsin and the University of Michigan, to name a few. Some of these differ considerably from INS.

The Air Force Academy game involves teams representing real nations, whereas the Northwestern simulation has nations that do not have counterparts in the real world. This does not mean, claims Alger, that students participating in INS find themselves in decision-making situations that are less real than those students who are simulating countries with real world names.

On the contrary, he says, both exercises attempt to simulate the real world. The advantage of contrived nations, according to the professor, is that they tend to "move the attention of the student away from particular nations and to focus it on the factors that affect the policies of nations and on the conditions that affect the relationship between these policies." [19]

Also, some game-makers note that when students role-play actual nations this often tends to stereotype their responses —that is, players tend to respond to the game situation the way they think a French or Russian decision-maker would respond, rather than spontaneously.

Unlike the Northwestern game, the MIT and Wisconsin

exercises simulate a particular kind of international relations situation—the crisis. Thus, players in the MIT and Wisconsin games find themselves in recreations of crises such as Berlin, Korea, Suez and Hungary. Not so players of INS, in which crises develop gradually out of national characteristics and the behavior of decision-makers.

Northwestern gamesters say the reason for this approach is that it draws attention to certain long-term characteristics of the international system, which, they add, are likely to be obscured by involvement in a short-term crisis.

Another difference between INS and the Air Force, MIT and Wisconsin games is that the latter all assign prominent roles to an umpire. Consider the rules for the umpire in the Air Force Academy simulation: "The umpire reserves the right to rule out any move by any state on the grounds of implausibility. Your moves in the game should be reasonably in character for the state which you are playing." The Northwestern effort does not have an umpire in this sense.

In INS, the "world" is designed so that decision-makers are in predicaments which in their basic characteristics are as much as possible like the real world. "Therefore," says Alger, "to the extent that this effort is successful, they can only do plausible things." At the same time, Northwestern educators worry that the intervention of umpires would add unreal actors—"gods"—to the game and thus imperil its use as an analytic tool for understanding the real world.

Northwestern's gamesters are not content with INS as it is, however. Recently, the school's scholars began working on a new exercise called an "international process simulation" that is far more complex than INS. "With this new simulation, we believe we'll end up with a far richer international environment," says Guetzkow.

Players in the international process game will find themselves dealing with many more variables than formerly. For one thing, the new game will include a number of international organizations, meaning countries will be dealing with each other on a number of different bi-lateral and multilateral bases. What's more, the game will include international business dealings that will require decision-makers to give far more weight to economic factors. Governments will send ambassadors to each other, and, on occasion, may expel them over international incidents. Spicing the game will be riots, demonstrations and anti-government protests. "Decision-makers will have to deal with a kind of international public opinion," says Guetzkow. "The simulation should be very exciting."

One obvious consequence of games is that they often lead to altogether new and different games. After being exposed to a simulation, several graduate students in political science at the University of Southern California in 1966 developed "Vietnam," a game simulating some of the complexities of that conflict. The game has actually been used in some high school and college classrooms in Los Angeles.

About the same time three divinity students, after playing one of many versions of INS currently in circulation, developed "Augustine City." After three months of model building, Robert C. Shukraft, now a Th.D. candidate at San Francisco Theological Seminary; John Moyer, now a church intern in Rumania; and William Relf, now completing a Ph.D. in political science at Claremont Graduate School, came up with the original version of the simulation.

Later in the 1966-67 school year the game was introduced in a course entitled *Pastoral Leadership in the Local Church*, taught by the Rev. Henry Kuizenga, a pastor in San Anselmo as well as a professor at the seminary. Dr. Kuizenga approved the experiment because he liked the simulation's "realism." According to Shukraft, the game is aimed at "bringing students closer to the reality that is the Church."

He describes the experiment as an attempt to use the classroom as a laboratory for those who will work in the church, "allowing the student to experience, understand and analyze the opportunities and frustrations of the local pastorate before he really enters it and must stand or fall on the quality of his decisions." [20] The game ties in naturally with the course, which, according to the seminary catalog, deals with the "pastor's changing role and functions; the multiple-staff ministry of laymen and of church groups, the administration of the local church program, and church self-study in relation to the community."

To incorporate these—and other—problems into the simulation, an imaginary community was created containing all the pressures that students will have to deal with later as pastors. And to overcome the resistance of initiates naturally hesitant to consume the mounds of material that go along with the game, the San Anselmo gamesters incorporated into the exercise a great deal of humor. "Humor helps get the students into the idea of the simulation," says Shukraft.

Consider Augustine City, second largest community in the state of New Sylvania. With its 750,000 inhabitants, the city is part megalopolis, part trade center for a thriving agricultural area. The city is well-endowed culturally, boasting two universities, seven playhouses, a museum, two art centers, a symphony orchestra, 22 movie houses, a major league baseball team (the Augustine City Angels) and a recent entry in the American Football League (the Augustine City Saints). The city is bisected by the Jordan River. One part of the town teems with industry, ethnic enclaves, slums and a Negro ghetto; a few miles away middle class neighborhoods flourish. The city is surrounded by wealthy suburbs.

Augustine City folk are church-going. Among the city's many religious institutions are eight Presbyterian churches, whose quandaries are aimed at reflecting those that plague real pastors. Each church has a distinct identity and a peculiarly unique set of troubles.

Take Bigdome Memorial Presbyterian Church, once the great church of Augustine City. But in recent years the great edifice has fallen upon hard times. Located in an industrial and troubled area, Bigdome has lost much of its membership and become a problem for the Presbyterian Church at large. Then there is Hollymammoth Presbyterian Church, which has been troubled by scandals and division in recent years.

Christchild church has been unable to keep up with a growing need for more buildings, while Big Fisherman church has had to contend with a beatnik colony in its area. Recently Rural church, once an uncomplicated country church, has been affected by the expansion of suburbia, so that it now joins older farm families with young suburbanites, teachers, engineers and workers. Located in the midst of the ghetto, Avant Garde church must deal with a congregation made up largely of slum-dwellers. Meantime, Gotrocks church flourishes in Lucre Manor, an elite suburb of Augustine City.

In the game, student teams must fashion strategies appropriate for easing the particular woes of the churches they represent. Each team consists of between two and six players, one of which is selected as pastor. The remaining team members act as staff members of the church, responsible to the pastor. The pastor's task is to direct his ministry, both as a continuation of the church's history and in relation to newly emerging situations.

Before play begins, each team must establish goals, decide upon priorities, and plan for the completion of objectives. The key to the game is its scoring mechanism. Pastors begin the game with 50 "influence" units, which are allocated to various church programs on the basis of ministerial perceptions of what constitute the congregation's "expectations" and "needs."

The trouble is, expectations and needs, or what the pastor perceives as such, aren't always in harmony. Yet the pastor's effectiveness is measured in part by the church's satisfaction with his job as minister. This means that to keep his congregation satisfied, the minister must allocate at least some of his influence units to programs he thinks will increase congregation satisfaction.

These church activities range from Christian education and adult fellowship programs to worship and youth programs. What units are allocated to develop these and other outside programs will depend on the nature of the congregation, or how the minister assesses the nature of the congregation.

The simulation is broken into an indefinite number of 60-minute time periods, each of which represents one quarter of the church year. During each period, the pastor makes decisions relating to allocation of his influence points and changes he plans to institute in the church. At the beginning of the next class period, players receive feedback on their decisions of the previous quarter, with detailed reactions to policies, sermons or programs, approval or rejection of proposed plans by members of the church, rising or declining attendance patterns, and general congregation satisfaction.

Basically, the student knows how well he is doing by checking the rise or fall of his "clergy influence units," which are the prime currency of the game. The CIU's—as they are known in the game's lexicon—are based on the premise that particular programs require the expenditure of so many units, a combination of time, energy, stature and effort. The scoring works so that a successful program returns to the player additional units, representing increased benevolences, renewed zeal of the congregation and so on. An unsuccessful program, however, reduces the balance of units, thus weakening the church's ability to carry on its program.

The outcomes are determined by a "hand calculator," which, like a computer, is programmed with certain cause-and-effect formulas. Operated by the game administrator, the calculator reflects the individual responses of each church to different decisions and strategies. That is, each church has a particular response pattern incorporated into the calculator, meaning that no one strategy is likely to elicit the same response from differing churches.

For the most part, teams compete against the model, rather than against each other. That is, teams are not in direct competition. Instead, they try to score well against a specific model, which is based on assumptions about how a particular congregation will respond to a particular strategy. Depending on the strategy, the minister's influence units rise or fall, reflecting the degree of congregation satisfaction or dissatisfaction with the minister's efforts. (The congregation is not represented in the game by players, but by pre-determined responses worked into the model. Players do, however, read a scenario that gives them a "feel" for their make-believe congregations.)

Even though they aren't supposed to, the various teams—many of which are playing in the same room simultaneously—do maintain an informal competition to see which one can accrue the largest number of satisfaction units. This may result in a distortion, since the purpose of the game really isn't to build up a high degree of congregation satisfaction.

Ideally, teams are supposed to generate just enough congregation satisfaction to enable them to lead the sometimes conservative congregations in desired directions, perceived by the pastors as essential to achieve certain religious or institutional goals. In this way conflict is built into the game, between minister and the congregation and between the church and the community. Thus, the game reflects the realistic strains that exist inside the church; pastors must use their ingenuity to find strategies that increase congregation morale while at the same time moving the congregation in a direction it may be reluctant to travel.

As the game proceeds, ministers usually find they must reconcile the purely theological values of their calling with the often intractable demands of practical survival. As explained by Shukraft, "It is the student's task to administer the work of his church with all the concomitant pressures, feeling the tug of his theology that called him to aid the Church in becoming redemptive." [21]

What are these pressures? Consider simply the problems confronting the player assuming the ministry of Bigdome, where the old minister, the Rev. Henry "Irish" Edsel, has just retired. As the game begins, the first trouble with which the new pastor must deal is an annual deficit of about $5,000 in church finances. For several years the deficit has been paid by the Greater Augustine Presbyterian Council (GAPC), but now the council is beginning to balk.

For one thing, the GAPC has expressed unhappiness with Bigdome's dwindling membership and the half-hearted efforts made by the church to reverse the trend. As a result, there is doubt whether the GAPC will continue absorbing Bigdome's yearly loss. So right off the new minister must deal with an interrelated quandary: A congregation whose decreasing numbers is aggravating an already strained financial situation.

In the early periods of the game, the new pastor finds the congregation apathetic. Membership stands at 610, down from a high of 1,000 in 1960. At the same time, the pastor finds that the congregation's malaise contrasts sharply with Bigdome's brilliant history. The church itself is a fine example of Baroque architecture. The high-domed ceiling of the sanctuary is vaulted and has seven golden chandeliers.

And Bigdome's pews are hand hewn cedars from Lebanon.

The organ—an original Skinfllint—was the finest of its kind when constructed. Each pew has a plaque naming famous members from Bigdome's history. The pulpit—made from wood used in an early covered wagon—hangs high over the pews.

Perhaps the source of Bigdome's problems is its downtown location in Augustine City. The city's growth and gradual industrialization has altered the nature of what once was the periphery of a relaxed residential area. The expansion of large buildings into the area has left few facilities for parking for members. The church's property is valuable, but so heavily mortgaged that members who wish to move the church don't know how to attack the problem. So far Bigdome has had no problems over ethnic differences. But as the game proceeds such problems may arise since a growing number of Puerto Ricans and Negroes are moving into nearby neighborhoods.

As with many simulations, "Augustine City" has a scenario describing the imagined history and personalities of the social processes and institutions replicated. Familiarizing himself with background materials on Bigdome, the new pastor finds that previous efforts to raise money got nowhere. For example, he reads that Dr. Edsel briefly considered raising money by renting church space to one of the following local groups: Augustine Home for Unwed Mothers, The Mattachine Society, Divorce Anonymous and Alcoholics Anonymous.

Dr. Edsel favored accepting these groups into the fellowship of the church. But he had to retreat when some members of the congregation threatened to leave on grounds the church would be used to support alcoholics, homosexuals, dope pushers and prostitutes. "The Body of Christ must be a pure and clean temple for God," said Isa Doolittle, an influential member of the congregation.

Complicating the pastor's problems is a widening generational gap in the church. For years benevolences have been left almost entirely to Bigdome's Women's Association. Mrs. Grace Archaic, president of the group, works hard but is constantly frustrated by the age differences of the members. The shrinking group of younger women in the church has objected strongly to being mixed with the older ladies. The conflict has curbed the association's fund-raising effectiveness.

Against this historical background, the new pastor must frame a strategy that will lift Bigdome out of the doldrums. But the minister also knows that he must approach the task cautiously since his congregation is a conservative one. From a theological standpoint, the minister may feel he should strengthen the young adult education and youth programs which have fallen into disuse.

At the same time, he knows he can't ignore the older folks, who dominate the congregation and whose support he'll need to solve the church's vexing financial problems. With a limited number of influence units to allocate, he's likely to compromise, spreading them equally among programs that favor older as well as younger members.

How the church is to be ultimately revived often is decided after the game is well underway, when the minister has built up sufficient congregation satisfaction to risk an unpopular program. Actually, there are few options open to the pastor. If he elects to keep the church where it is, he will have to devise "a really dramatic program that'll awaken the entire church," says Shukraft. "Such a program has doubtful prospects, since Bigdome is located in a deteriorating area."

Another of the ministry's options is to move the church to a suburban area. The idea has obvious appeal, but the minister will have to be deft in presenting the proposal since it could alienate older members who don't want to move. The minister also has the option of petitioning the GAPC for a permanent subsidy, but this seems an unlikely solution in light of the council's growing disaffection with Bigdome.

Finally, the minister may conceive of an alternative not programmed in the game. In this case the simulation's administrators would act as umpires, assessing the proposal on the basis of their subjective experience. In this way "Augustine City" resembles INS, in that both include a mix of "free" and "rigid" aspects of gaming.

As if the minister isn't already faced with enough problems, the game administrators arbitrarily introduce new ones as the game goes along. There are, for example, storms, strikes, elections and significant deaths. At one point players may be only outwardly grieved when a cranky but nevertheless rich parishioner dies, leaving a large sum to the church. But the parishioner's will includes one stipulation: The money must be used in part to decorate Bigdome's steeple with neon tubing. The minister's task is to find a way to qualify for the much-needed cash without agreeing to deface the steeple.

At other points administrators are likely to introduce civil rights and open housing demonstrations into the game. This presents the minister with an even more serious problem: He must act in a way that satisfies his own conscience as well as the sometimes conservative leanings of his flock. "Normally, players try to keep satisfaction levels high; this gives them room to maneuver," explains Shukraft.

But keeping parishioners happy isn't always possible. In one recent play of "Augustine City," a liberal-minded student acquiesced to the urgings of some members of his congregation to form an action group to participate in a rent strike that an administrator introduced into the game. The upshot: A large contingent of conservative members left the church, sharply reducing its membership.

When the congregation's satisfaction level decreases, "the players get very nervous," says Shukraft. "They feel the pressure very keenly. Frequently they back off from their liberal positions and become conservative for awhile. At such times they tend to spend several periods building up the church and their satisfaction levels."

Like INS and most other games, "Augustine City" places great emphasis on post-simulation discussion. When the exercise is over, players devote several sessions to analyzing the suitability of goals teams set for their churches and the effectiveness with which they implemented strategies.

Shukraft and his colleagues concede the game isn't without flaws. For one thing, they admit that the "influence unit" is a questionable abstraction. But they insist it's needed for two reasons: First, it forces the church staff to cover the entire church and to be specifically concerned with being a part of all the church does. Second, they claim it is a ready way of showing degree of acceptance of the staff by the congregation. Writes Shukraft:[22]

"It was assumed that many programs which would appeal to the idealistic student would fail unless he paid attention to the church. In other words, programs of change required precise planning and building, *in the context of the church being served.*

"What we tried to do was to bring the student an understanding of the ambivalent and often opposing pulls of what he may feel is right and what some church laymen expect. The contemporary pastor must understand that it is his job to develop the potential of the church, to bring the congregation together as a community; but he must also know that not all of his actions will meet with approval. Theological validity and pastoral success are not opposites; nor are they the same. The student needs to learn his own particular mixture of church growth and theological change."

Adding realism to the game is the "time" factor. Players constantly complain about being rushed and pushed without time to think. According to Shukraft, this is the way it really is on the job. "We also assumed that it is difficult to find time to think in long range terms; in short, that the pastor is always being pressed to answer immediate problems first," he observes.

Shukraft is particularly helpful in distinguishing between simulation and role-playing, which are often confused. He emphasizes that simulations are not an elaborate form of role-playing. "In role-playing the actor assumes another's identity, and must make decisions within that assumed identity—he is not himself," explains Shukraft. "In simulation the student steps into a situation in which he, as himself, must make decisions, bringing all of his theology, knowledge and experience to bear on the problem. The more real the model, the more involved the playing; the less real the model, the more the players analyze it with a view toward making it real."

What both INS and "Augustine City" have in common is that their problems and crises emerge slowly as a result of many rounds of play and interactions between players. But this is not the only kind of political game. Indeed, there are political simulations in which players find themselves embroiled in quagmires the minute they sit down at the game table.

Chapter 4

GAMING CRISES: FOUR DAYS IN DECEMBER

> "There is a play of possibilities and probabilities, of good and bad luck, which permeates every thread, great or small, of its web and makes war, of all branches of human activity, the most like a game of cards."—*Karl Von Clausewitz*

At a hastily-called emergency meeting, Cabinet members take seats around a large conference table to consider what to do about a far-away but worsening crisis that threatens to escalate into war. The session begins when the Chief Minister, after gravely eying the expectant officials, plunks down on the table a document marked Top Secret. The document, the Chief Minister's position paper on the situation, is read and passed around the table. It reads as follows:

"My foreign policy in the past rounds has been peaceful; however, this has not brought the required results. For that reason, I've moved troops into Inland. Both Nordo and New Zenith will want an explanation. The answer is a simple one: Our troops were placed in Inland to give us a bargaining point.

"New Zenith has agreed to let Hamil into the International Council if the Hamilians withdraw from Inland. New Zenith, however, has refused to withdraw her troops from Outland. The net result would be that Hamil is in the I.C., but Inland, who we must protect, is open to attack. If New Zenith will hold her bargain about Hamil, there is a good chance we can strike a bargain about withdrawing New Zenith troops from Outland while we withdraw our troops from Inland."

The document, of course, is fictitious; so are the countries. The deeply-involved ministers, simulating top-policy-makers for a nation called Transania, are in fact seniors at William Penn Charter School, a private school in Philadelphia. The situation, however, is not far removed from reality. The students are playing Dangerous Parallel, a game based on the Korean War developed by the Foreign Policy Association with the help of Abt Associates. (Based in New York, the association is the originator of the Great Decisions adult education program.)

The exercise is one of a growing number of political games that are rapidly finding favor in secondary schools across the country. Recently packaged by a commercial publisher, the FPA game is expected to be distributed widely to junior and senior high schools in 1968. Dangerous Parallel, however, is no mere political game. It falls into the category of "crisis game," a close relative of the war game which may or may not be completely manual. In such exercises, the crisis is "given" in the form of a scenario, which sets the stage for play. Unlike Professor Guetzkow's INS, in which tensions develop gradually out of moves made by participants, crisis games thrust players immediately nto a critical situation not of their own making. The actors then try to work their way out of the crisis within the framework of certain rules, usually as interpreted by a control team or a game administrator.

Simulating a critical point during the Korean War, Dangerous Parallel resembles in structure other crisis games designed specifically for high school students. One such exercise is CRISIS, a simulation of an international crisis over a mining area of vast importance to a fabricated "world" situation. CRISIS is a product of the Western Behavioral Sciences Institute's Project SIMILE, which has developed a panoply of games on grants from the Kettering Foundation. In addition to CRISIS, the La Jolla, California-based research group has devised PLANS, which simulates interest groups using influence to produce change in American society; NAPOLI, a simulation of the legislative process, and among other games, a manual version of INS for use by high school students. Both CRISIS and NAPOLI currently are being published and sold by Charles E. Merrill Book Co., a division of Bell and Howell Co., in Los Angeles.

Learning objectives of the recently-contrived FPA game are ambitious, to say the least. For one thing, Dangerous Parallel is aimed at teaching "the elements of a systematic analytical approach to international affairs, hoping to begin the creation of intellectual habits which will carry over into subsequent life," says the FPA. Another game objective is to teach a variety of things about how nations behave while, at the same time, conveying the nature of decision-making by "doing it rather than describing it," says an FPA official. A final objective of the exercise is to inculcate in students "empathy for cultures and institutions other than our own." Says one FPA spokesman:

"It seems very clear, for example, that the unaccustomed frustration of the student who, as representative of a small and weak country has tried in vain to get a great power to do something it is disinclined to do, is the basis for some real learning of an important kind: for Americans, especially, the feeling of belonging to a powerless nation is a revelation of an unfamiliar sort. Several major insights about how the world looks and feels to other nations are strong elements in this game—though they are likely to be 'learned' in a durable sense only if the teacher goes on to bring these lessons out explicitly in subsequent discussions where insights can be reinforced and related to other ideas."

According to the FPA, Dangerous Parallel is not to be taught as history, but, instead, is to be used as a means of learning about international relations. Thus, names of countries involved in the Korean crisis have been changed, and a fictitious map has been provided which vividly shows an imaginary part of the world. During play teachers are urged not to tell students what historic incident Dangerous Parallel represents. The reason for this, say FPA game-makers, is to spur free and realistic role-playing and to discourage playing "by the history book." That is, gamesters do not want students to be constricted in their thinking by the actual decisions that were made by history's real actors.

After the game has been played and discussed on its own terms, teachers then are encouraged to reveal what the historic situation and countries were. In post-simulation sessions, teachers are encouraged to lead students into an investigation of the real cultural and historic backgrounds of the countries and the conflict. FPA gamesters worry that the game cannot be taught as history without destroying its real usefulness, but they hope it can be "a springboard into what may be an exceptionally motivated exploration of history and cultures."

In Dangerous Parallel, 24 or more students at grade levels 10-12 play the roles of cabinet-level decision-makers dealing with a situation modeled closely on the Korean War. The game involves about eight days of class time, although the last few days are allotted to debriefing or post-simulation discussion sessions. Actual play may take up no more than four class periods on successive days, which was the length of time Penn Charter students devoted to the game. The exercise does not require special expertise or mathematical skill on the part of the teacher, or previous academic preparation by students. It is intended for average or better students, and for use in existing secondary school social studies courses.

While the game has been tried out at several schools, Penn Charter was the first to play it under the direction of a classroom teacher with a regular class. For about two weeks in December, 1967, 25 students from a world affairs class divided themselves into six teams, each having four players. Sitting at tables in the school's gymanisum, the teams represented six nations that had key roles in the Korean crisis. They included New Zenith, a rich, powerful land resembling the United States; Transania, a vast nation styled on the Soviet Union; Hamil, a large poor country suggestive of Red China; and Nordo, an equally poor country resembling India. Finally, there was Inland, modeled on North Korea, and Outland, modeled on South Korea.

Each team was comprised of a "chief minister," who was head of government, along with a cabinet made up of foreign, political, defense and economic ministers. As the game began, these governmental teams found themselves at a critical turning point in a political-military crisis that apparently had been going on for months. The background of the crisis was the invasion of Outland by Inland, whose forces had been driven back behind their own borders.

Students were handed FPA scenarios that summed up the "present situation" thusly: "The forces of New Zenith are poised on the border, ready to further pursue the weakened Inland troops. The Outland forces have already crossed the border, intent on destroying more of Inland's military capacity and on occupying as much of the Peninsula as possible. The New Zenith commander has recommended that his forces seize this opportunity to move to the borders of Hamil. All parties to the conflict and observers realize that no action taken can afford to risk the spread of conflict outside this theatre to the rest of the world. It is particularly important to avoid direct armed conflict between New Zenith and Transania, which almost certainly would escalate into a world war."

Play, however, does not begin immediately. Before attempting to deal with the crisis, the Penn Charter students were required to read a thick portfolio that was distributed to each team. The portfolio consists of a map, four pages of strategic briefing on the world situation, three pages profiling each team's particular country and the player's particular position in the government, and five pages dealing with decision-making. Included in the portfolio are 10 yellow pages supplying information aimed at helping students make their ultimate decisions.

In the strategic briefing, players learn that the "simulated world" is divided more or less into two power blocs, one of which is led by New Zenith and the other by Transania. According to the briefing materials, Inland is controlled by Transania while Outland is controlled by New Zenith. Hamil also is firmly in Transania's camp. Nordo, however, attempts to remain neutral, and tends to rely heavily on the International Council for settlement of disputes.

Known as the I.C., the Council is the game's version of the United Nnations. The briefing reports that the I.C. has become a forum "for debate between Transania and New Zenith, within which the two powers can propagandize the smaller nations." Hamil has not been admitted to the I.C. because the governments of New Zenith and its allies do not consider the government of that nation to be legitimate. Nevertheless, Transania and Nordo are campaigning for Hamil's membership. The I.C. resembles the UN in one important feature: Transania and New Zenith must agree before the I.C. can take any action, including admission of new members.

Since each portfolio is geared for a particular nation, the documents contain secrets that players are admonished to keep to themselves. These secrets have to do with assessments of the psychology, goals and possible actions of other countries in the "world" arena. For example, a member of the New Zenith team reads that Transania has "long borders historically vulnerable (and) recently has been dominating 'buffer' states on both East and West." Also, the New Zenith official finds that while Hamil is plagued by "desperate economic conditions, (its) military leaders feel the need for battles to give the newly unified country a national spirit and new leaders popularity." Hamil aims at driving "intruders from this part of the world," according to a high-level New Zenith estimate.

Guiding players in the action choices they will be making later in the game are the profiles describing the historical values and long-term interests of the nations they represent. These profiles also attempt to temper desired objectives with the short-term realities of the situation. Thus, a New Zenith policymaker reads that his long-term goal is the independence of Outland. At the same time, the profile warns "you want to be careful that, in trying to end the fighting, you do not get involved in a new world war." He is also charged with keeping Hamil out of the I.C.

The New Zenith officials also must labor under the uncertainty surrounding Hamil's possible responses. But if the same New Zenith official had access to the Hamilian profile that uncertainty would be diminished somewhat. Hamil's profile reads in part: "You want to make sure that at least a large part of the land Peninsula remains under control of a friendly nation, even if you have to step in and take it over yourself."

Throughout the emphasis is on realism; the profiles are real attempts to suggest the aspirations and interests of nations from their own point of view. There is in the game a minimum of moralizing. Inland's profile informs its ministers that "you feel that your system of government must win out in the entire Peninsula, because you must have tight control over all of the Land peoples so that they can build a strong nation."

Meantime, an Outlander reads in his own nation's profile that he should be grateful for New Zenith's support, without which Inland would have driven the "democratic" forces from the Peninsula. But the official is cautioned that this support may go just so far, since New Zenith has interests all over the world. The Outland profile reads: "If you are not able to persuade New Zenith to do what you want, you may have to try to work her into a position where she will have no choice except to back you up."

In the exercise policymakers are constrained in their choice of strategies by two factors: limited resources and limited ability to communicate with combatants. Each land in the game has a fixed amount of money and a fixed number of troops. Policymakers can move battalions, but only at a cost that eats into their financial reserves. Both Inland and Outland have large armies, but neither has the resources to move them without financial help from their allies. Lacking both money and troops, Nordo has only "influence" to make use of in the game.

Nations may opt for negotiations, but this is complicated by the need to communicate through third parties. To contact Hamil or Inland, neither of which it recognizes, New Zenith must go through either Transania or Nordo. This works to give Nordo a key role in the game. Only Transania, New Zenith and Nordo are members of the I.C., although new members can gain admission if both New Zenith and Transania are in agreement.

A final dash of authenticity is worked into the game by giving ministers a kind of bureaucratic point of view that reflects their specialty. Consequently, ministerial positions within nations have profiles just as do the nations themselves. For example, New Zenith's defense minister, pictured in the profile as skeptical of diplomacy, leans toward a demonstration of "military superiority" over Hamil and Transania. The chief minister, however, is informed that after listening to his various advisers, he must then "consider the total picture."

Students often spend the first two class sessions, each of which lasts about 45 minutes, familiarizing themselves with their nation's profile, their position in the government and the rules of the game. During this time no moves are made, although players are required to write a 200-word "white paper" on what they feel should be their government's policy in working out the crisis.

On the second day of the eight-day session players learn the "rules of the game." First, each country's chief minister receives a Decision Display Device (DDD) listing four policy or action choices permitted that country. That is, each nation must mull four possible courses of action during each round of play and then choose one. Players are warned by the Control, or game administrator, to regard as secrets the four choices, which are different for each country and range from extension of peace feelers to wholesale movement of troops.

Each of the team's four ministers are assigned to fully investigate the feasibility of each of the four policy alternatives in light of the current crisis. The students are helped in their evaluations by referring to a "planner's checklist" at the back of their portfolio. The checklist contains 10 policy-making factors students must consider before advancing or rejecting the action choice for which they are responsible.

The checklist asks the student to ponder the possible move in terms of how much it will cost, how it will affect the economies of adversaries and allies alike, whether it will be acceptable to public opinion at home and whether it will create important military risks for both the minister's country and its allies. Also, the checklist spurs students to question whether the move will really help the country attain its goals and, finally, examine whether the action may or may not be immoral in terms of the nation's deepest beliefs.

What is more, each factor is expanded upon by a full page

of analysis at the back of the portfolio. Here is how one such page reads:

> In working out an answer as to "whether this action will really help gain my country's goals," it will always be useful to think about these things:
>
> a. *What will be the results*—The consequences of this action?
> I need to do everything possible to figure out what will happen if my country does this. *Only after* thinking out probable results can I judge whether these are likely to help my country gain its goals.
>
> b. *Am I putting first things first?*
> There are *big goals* that affect my nation's strength, health, prosperity, safety or survival. Will taking this action choice:
> —help gain those big goals.
> —work against those big goals in some way?
>
> c. *Is this only a "sentimental" action choice?*
> That is, does it *really* gain goals, or does it just appeal to my country's emotions, its likes and dislikes, the wish to "get things over with," or find some easy way out? (*My* duty is to support *only* choices that gain goals!)
>
> d. My country has four action choices to select from. *Is this action choice better or worse than the others, for gaining my country's goals?*

The action begins on the third day, but not right away. For the first 10 minutes of the 45-minute session each nation's ministers discuss among themselves what course of action they will pursue and what "line" the chief minister should take in a "position statement" that will be made openly to all nations. The next five minutes is devoted to the reading of these brief position statements, which may or may not be an accurate reflection of a nation's intentions.

Following the position statements, Control announces the beginning of a Negotiation and Research Phase. During this brief period governments may negotiate with each other if they have diplomatic relations. Or they may do research in what is known as the Strategic File. The file contains 3x5 note cards with additional information about the country and its rleationships with other nations. The information is indexed by numbers corresponding to the Foreign Policy Factors on the Planner's Cheklist. For instance, a New Zenith minister worried about the morality of his country's involvement in the crisis, looks up the appropriate note card and finds this advice:

"Some people in New Zenith, including a few very important political figures, feel that it is morally wrong for New Zenith forces to be killing the people of another continent who have not threatened New Zenith soil. These people see no reason for New Zenith to attempt to control the destinies of smaller nations.

"Most people, however, are far more shocked by Inland's attack on Outland."

After the Negotiations and Research Phase, all ministers return to their countries. Then, for the next 10 minutes, the ministers discuss the results of negotiations and hear reports on possible action choices. They also must quickly prepare a new position statement that the chief minister will read to the whole group. After these statements, each country must make a policy choice, which is written on a sheet of paper and collected by Control.

During the session's final five minutes, Control calculates the result of the decisions made by the six nations. This is done very quickly. The game is programmed to permit 24 alternative choices—four for each of six nations—on each "move." Once action is called for by the teacher, all nations make their decisions simultaneously. Since all combinations of these 24 have been pre-programmed, the teacher is able to announce almost immediately the outcome of a round of six national decisions. Afterwards, players assess the results and begin to cope with the new situation which has come about.

As previously programmed, this combination of choices may result in one of nine "outcomes," ranging from a large indecisive battle and a negotiated truce to the outbreak of general war.

How the game works in practice was demonstrated during

four days of decision-making by Penn Charter students. After the first round of action choices, the Move Outcome calculated by Control was a temporary ceasefire. This developed despite the fact that Hamil moved its troops into Inland while Inland and Outland began moving forces towards each other. Transania, however, proposed a peace conference, as did Nordo. New Zenith kept its troops stationary and extended peace feelers.

Despite the inconclusiveness of play, some of the students apparently felt they were learning something in the area of *realpolitick.* Consider the thoughts of the Transanian chief minister (whose secret papers have been available to the author). He wrote:

"After the first round I find that I have learned some important points: (1) Don't play hunches without doing proper research, (2) Don't be afraid of your own power, (3) Don't put too much trust in your friends.

"I am going to recommend our giving $4 to $8 billion in financial aid to Inland. This will help retain their loyalty without giving them enough of a cash reserve to mount an offensive. The battalions of Transanian troops are still on the Inland border. I hope I won't have to commit them.

"Hamil has been warned that if they don't consult us before making a policy decision, their aid will be terminated. I hope this will make them listen to us. However, I still want Hamil in the I.C.

"Nordo will act as our courier to Outland, and we are making some border agreements.

"Perhaps today's soft line policy did not bring the expected results, but I will not abandon it entirely. I do intend to follow a harder line in the future."

On the second day of decision-making, which was preceded by the usual round of negotiations and speech-making, the world situation at least seemed a little brighter. The Move Outcome for the round was a "negotiated truce with temporary border as the demarcation line." This outcome was calculated after both Inland and Outland softened their moves. Inland, for example, offered to negotiate while Outland stopped the forward movement of its troops. Hamil remained the most truculent member of the world community, demanding I.C. membership as a precondition to a peace conference. Transania, New Zenith and Nordo maintained their earlier "soft line" positions.

After the round the Transanian chief minister mused:

"Our policy [tomorrow] will be in a more or less 'play by ear' style. I think we can get Hamil in the I.C. with veto power. Inland cannot start another war. Neither can Hamil; so much for a world war.

"Our country has never had any compunction about backing out of an agreement. I therefore see little to fear in temporarily recognizing Outland. If this will help get Hamil in the I.C., I see nothing wrong with it.

"I want a return to the original situation in Inland-Outland. This will give us time to regroup and wait for a more advantageous time to conquer Outland."

The fragility of the truce did not go unnoticed by Nordo, whose foreign minister glumly reported to colleagues:

"At this point there is a deadlock of the nations. The recently arrived at truce will not last. To attain any lasting peace, Nordo should try to side with New Zenith as much as we can without sacrificing our neutrality. The reason is that New Zenith will not let Hamil in the I.C. because then she will be outnumbered. Thus if we can get New Zenith to think we are with them, then our vote would neutralize Hamil's. This should cause a considerable result if Nordo is not committed too far. I still think we must remain neutral, but we should try to accomplish my plan in a subtle manner."

These intrigues did nothing to improve the international climate in the third round when the truce, in State Department parlance, came unstuck. Transania, departing from its peaceful posture, moved troops into Inland, thus creating the danger of a direct confrontation between the super powers. Inland massed its troops on the Inland-Outland border. Even Nordo, which earlier considered leaning toward New Zenith, adopted the Hamil line, insisting on Hamil's admission to the I.C. as a precondition for a peace conference.

New Zenith, meantime, continued to extend peace feelers while keeping its forces in place. Outland proposed a peace conference to negotiate the unification of Outland and Inland. The programmed outcome of these six moves was another temporary ceasefire.

It was at this point that Transania's chief minister explained that he moved troops into Inland to give Transania a "bargaining point"—a strengthened hand in dealing with New Zenith. Transania's short-term objective was twofold: Spur New Zenith to withdraw from Outland while at the same time gaining Hamil's membership in the I.C. with veto powers. The success of the Transanian ploy was to be tested early in the fourth and final round of play during negotiations at the I.C. After a hard bargaining session, the Transanian ruler reported back to his ministers that the effort to intimidate New Zenith had not worked. He submitted the following position paper:

"We have failed in Inland; with New Zenithian troops in Outland we can't possibly hope to conquer the land Peninsula at this time. I believe we should sue for peace and demand that the borders be returned to their original position. To stress our sincerity I will order six battalions of our troops (back) to the Inland border.

"I am afraid of Hamil. I believe if Outland makes much

more progress, Hamil will fully commit herself to a third world war. Our foreign minister is going to try to stall Hamil. I do, however, want Hamil in the I.C.

"Nordo must be kept either neutral or on our side. If New Zenith were able to influence Nordo we would wind up with a long unfriendly border. I plan to to use Nordo as our courier in this conflict. To gain Nordo's confidence we are going to make treaties with her which will settle her fears about 'border adjustments.' "

Even though seemingly thwarted in its prime objective, Transania's hardline policies nevertheless weren't without impact. Indeed, that country's surprise movement of troops into Inland brought matters to a head, convincing even New Zenith that the situation was in danger of getting out of hand. Fearing the outbreak of a "world" war, New Zenith and the other nations agreed to a general peace conference that included even Hamil. The result was what appeared to be a general peace settlement.

New Zenith's perception of the dangers prompted its ministers to a major concession—entry of Hamil into the I.C., although as a non-veto member. Old China Hands may wince, but New Zenith wasn't alone in making concessions. Out of the conference came a peace agreement in which Hamil agreed to withdraw her troops from Inland in three months. Both Transania and New Zenith agreed to withdraw their forces within nine months. Also, Inland and Outland signed a truce and, finally, the six nations established a demilitarized zone that would be patrolled by Nordo. A seeming peace, but afterwards students confided to teachers they felt war would have broken out had the game continued.

The simulation experience was capped by two days of debriefing, in which students attempted to evaluate moves made during the four days of play. Theoretically, the teacher may at this point inform students that the exercise was modeled on the Korean War. Very early in the game, however, most players had figured this out, which is "a real problem with the game," concedes Allan Brown, who heads Penn Charter's history department and helped conduct the game.

The danger, says Brown, is that "if students know in advance the historical event being simulated, they will let their behavior become stereotyped. That is, they may act in a way they think is 'right' in terms of the country they represent, rather than try to work their way out of the crisis on their own." Brown's fears seemed justified during the general peace conference when the Transanian delegate, apparently recalling Khruhschev's performance at the United Nations, pulled off his own shoe and banged it on the conference table.

Another problem crept into the game when some students seemed to perceive the 18-year-old crisis in terms peculiar to the late 1960's. "Players representing Hamil (China) and Transania (Russia), no doubt aware of the current Sino-Soviet split, tended to act as if there was a greater split between the two countries than actually existed at the time. The Russian and American players also seemed to move toward a kind of detente, which certainly wasn't realistic at that time," says Brown.

Finally, Brown questions whether students have open to them a sufficient number of action choices. Despite these drawbacks, the Penn Charter teacher, who had a hand in developing the exercise, is convinced such experiences have value. "Gaming isn't an answer by itself; a game is purely a motivational tool," declares Brown, who notes that for the exercise to be meaningful it should be tied in with reading and other follow-up activities after the game.

Students particularly spurred by games "tend to be the apathetic middle," observes Brown. "These students get really enthusiastic. The better students sometimes feel a little let down by the experience." There's no question that most of the Penn Charter players found themselves deeply absorbed in the simulation while it lasted.

A case in point is provided by the vigour with which some students hurled themselves into espionage, which was permitted under rules of the game. Players were expressly forbidden from invading each other's desks or lockers. Not surprisingly, one portfolio soon disappeared, although it was later returned. Still, the victimized delegation was painfully aware that at least one other team knew all their secrets.

After this incident students were charged with carrying their portfolios with them at all times. Despite such precautionary measures one ingenious spy managed to remove several pages of vital data from a number of portfolios. Visibly peeved, Brown told the students that the game could not go on without them. A short time later he found the missing pages in his office, the spy having returned them as deftly as he took them.[1]

The apparent limitations of Dangerous Parallel haven't prevented the game from spreading far beyond the classroom. Not only has the game been packaged for use by interested high schools, but adults also are getting in on the act. For example, early in 1968 Boston's new UHF educational station, WGBX-TV, ran the game live over a five-week period, although with one difference. Enough time was allowed between moves to permit viewers to phone in their own "action choice" recommendations.

"If you can get people actively involved," says program executive producer Richard H. Lee, "then you can get them to better understand the essence of international politics."[2] For their part, viewers seemed unawed by the complexities of world politicking. When fighting broke out on the

Inland-Outland border during the first show, station phone lines were jammed by enthusiastic arm-chair experts calling in advice.

An extra element of drama was added by the method of selecting players for each team. The U.S. desk, for example, was manned solely by Negroes, while intellectuals handled Russian decision-making. India was played by foreign students, local housewives controlled the two Koreas, and clergymen took the part of China. Whatever the reasons, these adult players proved less prudent than their William Penn counterparts. In the fifth and final round a nuclear war was triggered when the Russian team moved its troops into Korea.

Looking into the future, Northwestern's Guetzkow foresees the time when players from a number of nations will participate in the INS or some other simulation. The game probably would emanate from an American television studio and be bounced off Telstar to several countries. "There's no reason why participating in a simulation should be limited to one country," says the professor.

Strongly reminiscent of INS and Dangerous Parallel is CRISIS, developed by WBSI's Project SIMILE, one of 15 major projects at the California research institute. With an annual budget of about $450,000—most of which is supplied by Federal research grants and contracts—this "think tank" of about 72 scholars does basic research in psychology and the other behavioral sciences.

Project SIMILE's games are now used in about 10 states, a number certain to increase since Bell & Howell is marketing two of them—NAPOLI and CRISIS. Like INS, CRISIS—whose materials cost about $35 for 25 students—is built around a theoretical model. According to Hall Sprague, executive director of WBSI: "The model makes it possible for the simulation participants to encounter 'reality'; they make decisions which are 'fed into' the model, and the model produces 'feedback' for the participants, outlining the consequences of their decisions."

Also like INS, CRISIS involves a wholly fictitious situation that does not refer to any existing countries or any historical crisis. The game's "world" is made up of six nations: Axiom, Burymore, Camelot, Dolchaveet, Ergosum and Fabuland. Each nation in this non-computer game has four decision-makers. Other students serve as messengers for the written communications between nations, or as reporters for the "World Times," a newspaper published between sessions. Finally, a few students serve as analysts who manipulate the mathematical formulae which determine results and repercussions of each nation's activities. The game is played in a room large enough to accommodate each nation's table, all of which are grouped in a kind of circle. The game's director and analysts sit at tables off to one side.

The game resembles Dangerous Parallel in that it begins in the middle of a crisis, albeit a purely hypothetical one. Rather than a struggle over Korea, CRISIS involves a six-nation contest for Dermatium, a mythical mineral central to survival in the "world." Each nation's objective is to obtain the rare mineral for its people while at the same time avoiding destruction of the nation. And, of course, each decision maker must maintain himself in office.

"Yours is no simple task," the instruction manual warns the player, "since if you assume an aggressive position, your nation may become involved in a war. On the other hand, if your people are denied access to the Dermatium, you will likely be thrown out of office by the ballot or in a revolution."

Here is a profile of the crisis situation that was distributed to Ergosum:

"The rare element Dermatium is mined in the Rhu Day Valley which borders the two countries of Ergosum and Fabuland. Until now an uneasy peace held together by the Peaceheard Pact has allowed both countries to mine this element. Several times during the past few years each of the countries had disputed the right of the other to use the mines, but on every occasion an agreement has been reached and fighting avoided.

"Dermatium is a volatile element and thus is very dangerous to mine. Until recently it was used primarily in the production of skin cream. Last week, however, scientists discovered that by shooting Dermatium through the dried digestive tracts of monkeys which had been fed iodized salt, a new synthetic substance, Balonium, could be created, one pound of which contains energy sufficient to run all of man's present machines for the next 10,000 years; or, if used destructively, enough explosive power to destroy the world. This discovery obviously has increased the value of the Rhu Day Valley and is a major factor in the crisis which is now developing, as evidenced by these recent incidents reported by the World Times:

"1. On the night of April 2, an explosion ripped through the Ergosum portion of the Dermatium mine, blocking tunnels and destroying machinery. Although there has been no official announcement or statement, it is generally felt by Ergosum intelligence experts that the Fabuland government masterminded the explosion.

"2. The Ergosum Air Force has reported Fabuland reconnaissance planes over the airspace of Ergosum. The chief strategist of the Air Force feels that the Fabuland planes are selecting targets for an impending attack.

"3. Ergosum reconnaissance planes report that Fabuland troops are bivouacked in the hills just beyond the Rhu Day Valley.

"4. Persistent rumors state that Camelot and Dolchaveet are giving undercover aid to Fabuland in the hopes that they will receive Dermatium after a Fabuland takeover of the mines.

"5. Many world leaders are wondering if Axiom and Burymore will come to the aid of Ergosum as they have in the past."

The game begins with an emergency session of the World Organization, which continues for a predetermined number of sessions. Each nation sends a delegate to the WO session while other policymakers figure their nation's relative strength, which is measured in BRs (Basic Resources) and include everything from manpower to agricultural productivity to ammunition. During the game, participants find that the prudent allocation of these resources are just as important as good diplomacy.

During a recent play of the game in a San Diego high school, pressure built up as the game progressed. There were urgent calls for "Messenger! Messenger!" as time ran out. A harried decisionmaker, stymied over how to allocate his BRs, was interrupted by demands for aid from an insistent ally who threatened to join a rival bloc if help was not forthcoming immediately. Just as he dropped his calculations to form a reply, a message was received from the nation's WO delegate that a rival power had turned suspicious and was threatening war. Such incidents are typical, say gamesters.

Not so typical, however, was the incident at a North Carolina school, where students continued their "playing" of CRISIS well beyond the conclusion of that day's session. Worried about their team's position in the simulated world arena, three decision makers collared the chief decision maker of a not-so-friendly neutral in the school cafeteria. The three students pressed the other player to join his team with theirs in an international alliance. Their bait wasn't economic or military aid; instead, they offered three untouched desserts.

Despite such blandishments, CRISIS, like other political games can end in a variety of ways—from peace or a nervous truce to a general war.

For those who eventually tire of international squabbles there is NAPOLI, which deals with power struggles in the domestic area. NAPOLI (national politics) turns students into legislators representing fictitious districts and one of two political parties: The American Traditionalist Party (ATP) or The American Modernist Party (AMP). At a party caucus, "legislators" elect party leaders and decide which of 11 bills—supplied with the game—should be brought before the legislature. At a regional caucus, the politicians discuss how the bills will affect their various constituencies and what action should be taken.

Then, in a classroom setting, a simulated version of the House of Representatives meets. First, members of the majority party elect the Speaker and, secondly, vote on the order in which the 11 bills will be considered. Once a bill is before the House, legislators are allowed to speak for or against and try to gather support for their position. After four bills have been voted on, the Game Administrator informs players of their chances of re-election, an assessment based on voter sentiment and the party's record of bills passed and defeated.

After all 11 bills have been voted on, the Director informs lawmakers whether or not they have been re-elected. This calculation, however, is based not only on voter sentiment and the party record. As will be explained later, re-election depends in part on chance—represented by a roll of dice.

Before the game begins, the Director assigns players to represent eight geographical regions—such as Agra, Baha, etc.—in a way that gives each region a fairly equal number of members. Students are allowed to choose their own parties, although some may have to be assigned to assure a split roughly 55%/45% between the majority and minority parties. The game begins when the Director permits regional groups to assemble in various parts of the classroom for a brief caucus. After a few minutes, the Director announces the beginning of the party caucuses, which last about 15 minutes. In these sessions a Speaker is elected, and then the Director calls for the first session of the House. WBSI gamesters recommend that the parties sit on opposite sides of the classroom—or legislature—with an aisle between them. The Speaker, usually but not always a student, then begins running the simulation.

By the time the first session begins the player has received a Legislator's Record Form—on which will be recorded his party's record on each bill—and a sheet indicating the results of an opinion poll taken in the legislator's region. Thus, the player knows in advance how his constituency feels about the 11 bills, the contents of which are explained in a participant's manual.

Of the 11 bills, four are backed by the ATP and another four by the AMP; three have bipartisan support. Before play actually begins students must familiarize themselves with each of the bills as well as the philosophy of their party. The ATP, for example, is described as the party of conservatism, endeavoring "to control the forces of change in such a way as to conserve the best elements of the past." The AMP, meanwhile, is described in the player's manual as the party of liberalism, standing for "the fullest and most free development of individual rights and opportunities in a way that harmonizes with the realities of present and future social conditions."

During the legislative session, the Speaker allows two "pro" and two "con" speeches—each of which may last no longer than one minute—on each bill before the House. Then the Speaker permits a five-minute free discussion period in which "members of the House" mingle freely, seeking support for or opposition to bills that interest them. During this time they are allowed to horsetrade and make various "deals" to get certain bills passed.

Typical of the measures for which ATP members seek support is Bill No. 1, which would reduce the maximum corporate income tax rate to 40 per cent from 48 per cent. Another ATP-sponsored bill would withdraw the United States from the United Nations. Meantime, the more liberal AMP politicos are stumping for measures to reduce the work week to 35 from 40 hours and to double federal aid to education to $3 billion from $1.5 billion.

The simulation ends when all bills have been passed or defeated, although recesses occur after action has been taken on four measures. After the votes have been taken the Game Director acts as scorekeeper. He computes two kinds of score—regional score and party score. The regional score is calculated by comparing the voter sentiment in the legislator's region on each bill with the legislature's action on the bill. The percentages of voters for and against the bills and the ratings they give to the bills are considered. If the computations yield a positive number, the player receives a "plus" regional score.

The participant's party score is determined on the basis of a comparison between the two parties. That is, if the player's party has passed two bills and the other has passed none, he receives a "plus" party score and the other party will receive a "minus" party score. Those players receiving pluses on both their regional and party scores stand an excellent chance of re-election. But re-election is in doubt for those players who end up receiving a combination of pluses and minuses. Ultimately, however, re-election depends on the roll of dice, whose outcomes are geared on the basis of a probability formula to favor players with the highest regional and party scores.

Before the game students are told their goal is "to perform in the legislature in such a way as to maximize your chances of re-election." Gamemakers do not contend that this is the only motive present in politics; rather, they argue its importance must be exaggerated so players can better understand the legislative process. Nevertheless, not all students "play the game" according to this rather arid stricture. Indeed, some insist on "voting their consciences" despite the electoral consequences, observes WBSI's Hall Sprague.

As the WBSI and Foreign Policy Association games suggest, not all exercises have a decisive winner. Some economic games measure success strictly in monetary or numerical terms. In NAPOLI, what counts is a quantitative score that means re-election. In the Family Game, a Johns Hopkins developed game that will be discussed later, success is measured in "satisfaction points." But in the FPA's Dangerous Parallel the "winner" is not so easily defined. "While the players do suffer monetary and troop losses, success in play is determined by whether the crisis has ameliorated or worsened by the decisions made and their consequent outcomes," says an FPA spokesman.[3]

Even though Dangerous Parallel, CRISIS and NAPOLI are not computerized, they do fall into the category of rigid games, since the outcomes of all moves that can be made during play are programmed in advance. Consequently, they have been criticized by some participants for not allowing a sufficient number of alternatives, or options for decision-makers faced with sticky situations.

Like those at FPA, La Jolla gamesters place heavy emphasis on what happens after the simulation. After a round of CRISIS, for example, Sprague urges teachers to hold discussions in which students can challenge the "consequences" built into the game. To make the exercise meaningful, he suggests students list a few important turning points in CRISIS and try to guess how similar developments occurred or are occurring in the real world. After all, claims Penn Charter's Allan Brown, "the whole point of games is to capitalize on the motivation they create. They certainly aren't ends in themselves."

While not ends in themselves, gamemakers argue the exercises have surprising advantages that aren't always obvious at first glance. For one thing, simulations may affect "the social setting for learning" in the classroom, says Sprague.

In an exhortation to teachers, Sprague claims: "The changes in physical surroundings alone—chair shuffling, grouping, etc.—may produce a more relaxed, natural atmosphere between you and your students later on. The involvement of the students may cause them to drop their usual facades, thus opening up better communications between themselves and you. And maybe simulations—like any new technique—will cause you to look at your usual teaching methods with a more critical eye."[4]

For the most part, games like CRISIS, NAPOLI and Dangerous Parallel are aimed at the average or better-than-average student. But some adventurous gamesters and educators have found that games are often particularly effective with underachievers and slow learners. At the same time, some games seem to naturally lend themselves to the educational experiments that for years were no more than gleams in reformers' eyes. How games have been adapted for special categories of student has implications that extend far beyond the classroom.

Chapter 5

GAMES FOR THE QUICK AND THE SLOW

> "Life must be lived as play, playing certain games, making sacrifices, singing and dancing, and then a man will be able to propitiate the gods, and defend himself against his enemies, and win in the contest."—*Plato*, "Laws."

Nova Olympic ☆

Each spring since 1966, dozens of high school students from across the country have converged on Nova High School in Fort Lauderdale, Fla., for the school's annual Olympic games. But the activities at Nova's sumptuous spread—part of the 545-acre South Florida Education Center—have had little to do with the usual athletic exertions conjured by the word Olympics. Instead, Olympic participants shun the rigors of the track for the comforts of the classroom: They play games like Equations, a mathematics exercise devised by a Yale law professor, in an experiment to determine whether strategy games can have an influence on the adolescent as pervasive as that of athletic programs.

Nova public schools—which combine elementary and secondary grades in a single complex—are among a small but growing number of schools attempting to translate into actual programs the theories of James Coleman, Jerome Bruner and other educators who believe games can improve the academic climate in classrooms. Recognizing that high school athletes generally are accorded recognition and prestige by their peers while scholars are less "acceptable," Robert W. Allen, director of Nova's three-year-old Academic Games Project, declares that the Nova Olympics are aimed at restructuring this "value perspective." In time, through competitive use of a panoply of games, Allen hopes the school achievement of adolescents will be improved by "altering the structure of values and rewards evidenced in many schools."

The Nova experiment reflects the unmistakable influence of Coleman who, along with seven other educators, serves on the advisory board of Nova's Academic Games Project, which is operated in conjunction with nearby Nova University. Some of the roughly two dozen games used at Nova have been developed at Johns Hopkins' Department of Social Relations, whose researchers have been putting together "games with simulated environments" since 1962. But a good many of Nova's games are a product of the Academic Games Project's own efforts. The result is that its storeroom burgeons with a wide range of games that have penetrated nearly every level and content-area taught at the Nova complex, a highly experimental set of schools part of the Broward County public school system.

Funded with the help of the Ford Foundation and the U.S. Office of Education, the Nova project is a three-stage effort to: (1) Integrate academic games into the entire curriculum and oganize competition at the classroom, intramural and interscholastic levels; (2) Evaluate the effects of the games on comprehension, recall, analysis and synthesis of subject matter, and upon the attitudes and achievements of slow and gifted students; and (3) Spread the academic games concept through course outlines, teachers' guides, instructional films, in-service training of teachers, and publicized competition.

As part of its research program, Nova gamesters currently are testing three main hypotheses:

1. Students who participate in academic games built around the key concepts of the course curriculum will have greater long-term retention of these concepts than students who do not participate in the games.

2. Students in experimental classes will evidence an improvement in attitude towards the course following the introduction of the games.

3. Students who excel in the academic games, especially those who are selected to participate in intramural and interscholastic competition, will increase in peer acceptance and show an accompanying increase in self-acceptance.

Nova researchers probably will spend years working on these ambitious and so far unconfirmed hypotheses. Meantime, the games project has been remarkably successful integrating the exercises into Nova's curriculum and spreading their use far beyond Florida.

Equations, for example, is used by most mathematics teachers from Suite A to Suite D (grades 1-6) at the ungraded Nova Elementary School as an optional enrichment activity. The game is also used by the slowest mathematics classes for seventh and eighth-year students at Nova High. Fifth and sixth-year pupils at Nova Elementary School play a game called Wff'n Proof to learn propositional logic.

Both games were developed in the early 1960's by Layman Allen, associate professor of law at Yale University and brother of Nova's Robert Allen. Layman Allen began work on the games after receiving a grant from the Carnegie Corp. for a project called ALL—Accelerated Learning of Logic.

How do these games work? Pupils begin Wff'n Proof by competing in small groups to make Wffs, or well-formed formulas, with lettered cubes. After learning the definition of a Wff, which is the letters or combination of letters constituting correct formulas, players progress at their own speed through a series of 21 games, each of which is more difficult than the preceding one. Hopefully, this leads to a grasp of propositional calculus and mathematical logic.

Equations requires players to use cubes marked with numbers and symbols to form equations. The idea of the exercise is to spur students to develop skill in abstract reasoning and logical thinking, speed and accuracy in computing, and understanding of the basic concepts of mathematics.

The Nova project also makes available a mathematics game called On-Sets, aimed largely at "developing readiness" in pre-school youngsters for the learning of set theory. In the game, players learn to deal with the basic combinations of classes, including union, intersection, exclusion, inclusion, equivalence and negation.

In 1966, a group of 80 Hollywood, Fla., youngsters of ages 3, 4 and 5 were introduced to On-Sets. During the first 45-minute session, "every youngster was able to recognize the union and/or the intersection of sets," according to Robert Allen. During a two-month period in which the games were used once a week, Allen says the youngsters were able to recognize the difference and complement of sets.

Nova's games are by no means limited to mathematics students, however. The seventh-year English class and an eighth-year social studies unit at Nova play The Propaganda Game, developed by Robert Allen and his long-time friend, Lorne Greene, star of "Bonanza" on television. To score well in the game, students must identify in the process of playing various techniques of persuasion, such as faulty analogy, attacking a straw man, prejudice, quotation out of context, folksy appeal and others.

Another Nova-developed game played in social studies classes is Euro-Card, aimed at giving players a mental picture of the relative size, shape and location of the European nations.

Among Nova's other games are Traffic, a simulation game in which players encounter driving situations similar to those one confronts while operating a motor vehicle; Investigation, aimed at spurring players to recognize common errors that are made in scientific inquiry; and The Real Numbers Game, an exercise involving the number systems of integers and natural, rational, irrational and real numbers. Object of the game is to arrive at the largest collection of numbers within a given system by manipulating randomly-allocated numbers and symbols.

Complementing the Nova-developed exercises are a host of games contrived by Johns Hopkins' researchers, whose gaming activities have been financed by a series of Carnegie Corp. grants since 1962. Nova is by no means the only outlet for Johns Hopkins' simulations, which have been distributed to dozens of schools across the country. One researcher estimates that the number of Johns Hopkins' games packaged and sold may approximate 10,000. Of that number, several thousand have been purchased by national 4-H Clubs for distribution to local branches.

A few of Johns Hopkins' more sophisticated games are, nevertheless, used by the Nova project. They include The Game of Democracy, a legislative game resembling in some ways NAPOLI, and Life Career, one of Johns Hopkins' most widely distributed exercises. In the latter, student teams, or single participants "play" a hypothetical individual as he moves through life and makes decisions about education, jobs, marriage, and other matters. The team that makes the most realistic decisions, given the qualities of the "individual" whose life they are managing, wins the game.

A particularly versatile game, Life Career has been used successfully at many levels of age and ability. Indeed, both Baltimore and San Diego schools have used Life Career and other games to motivate slow learning students. The Pennsylvania Advancement School in Philadelphia currently is using Life Career in an experiment to motivate underachieving eighth grade students. Palo Alto, Calif., public schools recently began using Life Career to help interest sometimes apathetic students in job possibilities beyond those that would normally occur to them.

While more widely used than most, Life Career is like other Johns Hopkins games in that all are aimed at narrowing the discrepancy between the adult and teenage worlds. Some others used at Nova are Consumer, Community Disaster and the Family Game.

As explained by Johns Hopkins' gamesters, the community disaster game is designed to provide "familiarity with the kinds of reactions a person undergoes in a crisis situation and the kinds of strategies that are most effective in solving such a crisis." In the game, which can be played by six to nine players, students sit around a schematic "map" which gives the location of police station, fire department, industrial and residential areas of a medium sized town, with a network of roads connecting them. This is how the game works in practice:[1]

"When the game starts, players are informed that a catastrophe has occurred in an unspecified part of the town and that people may have been injured and property destroyed. Each player is given a role in the simulated community, including his location at the start of the game, the relatives and friends he has in the community, his job, and any special obligations or interests such as property owned. Everyone is therefore anxious about the fate of persons and things he cares for.

"To alleviate their anxiety, players may try to find out what has happened by listening to radio broadcasts, telephoning relatives, friends or agencies, or by moving around the community (each such activity requires expenditure of a given number of 'energy units'). In the course of their activity, players will see how much of what subsequently happens in the community (e.g., telephone or road jams, the operation or non-operation of key public agencies) are the direct consequence of their own decisions and actions.

"When players learn where the disaster area is and the extent of the damages, community organization becomes imperative. To evacuate relatives in the disaster area requires entering that area, and this requires the intervention of the department of public works to clear the roads, of the fire department to control any blazes, of the police station to control road jams, etc. If the community cannot organize itself quickly or efficiently enough, the disaster can spread, possibly causing damage beyond repair (in such a case everyone 'loses').

"At the end of the game, the players elect from among the three with the lowest total 'anxiety' score the one who did most for the community. The winner is then the player who was both most efficient in committing his own energies and most visibly cooperative in helping his neighbors overcome the disaster."

In Consumer, which calls for 8 to 16 players, participants play the roles of consumers, credit and loan managers, and salesmen. The game's objective is to teach adolescents about the economics and problems of installment buying.[2] This is done by placing the students in a "simulated environment" in which situations arise not unlike those in real life. Thus, players must weigh the added cost of financing a purchase against the additional value to them of having the item now. They must also compare the interest rates charged by different financial institutions, such as banks and personal loan companies.

In the game, students learn that it's often a wise strategy to defer immediate consumption pleasures in order to improve their credit rating or put their economic affairs on a sound basis. During the game, consumers receive a monthly income with which they may buy certain products. They receive satisfaction or utility points for each item purchased.

But the exercise is structured in such a way that the desired item for purchase may be at its greatest value precisely when the consumer is short on cash.

The consumer is also plagued by random events, such as accidents or unemployment. Thus, players are often faced with the need to borrow, to buy a product or pay some emergency bill. The winning player is he who maximizes his utility points while at the same time minimizing credit or interest charges for which he is penalized.

The Family Game, which may be played by up to 10 young persons, attempts to simulate the interaction between a parent and an adolescent son or daughter in which there are opposed attitudes on certain domestic issues. Gamesters explain that the conflict is presented within a context of rules which reflect the structure of power and interdependence in the family. The game is aimed at giving participants some understanding of this structure and aiding them to shape effective strategies for handling such conflicts.

In one version of the game, the child has two behavior alternatives for each of five issues that must be resolved. One alternative is preferred by the parent, the other by the child. However, the strength of preference varies from issue to issue. The parent's score is determined solely by the child's eventual acts—which are indicated by the child on a playing board. The child's score is determined by his own behavior and by whether he receives any parental punishment.

The game consists of several rounds, each of which begins with a few minutes discussion between parent and child. At this point, they try to reach agreement on how the child will behave. When the two cannot reach agreement on an issue, the parent gives an order to the child on how he is to behave. Afterwards, the child selects his behavior; he may violate agreements or disobey orders. The parent, however, can then administer punishment, which causes points to be subtracted from the child's score.

In the scoring, parent and child do not compete against each other, but parent against parents and child against children who are playing at other boards. In effect, gamesters claim the exercise is intended to demonstrate that domestic peace can be established by a system of bargaining in which both sides recognize the wisdom of compromise and adherence to agreements.

It is this panoply of games, then, that constitute a substantial portion of Nova's game program. They are by no means used simply as teaching aids. Indeed, many of the games have been adapted for use in a program of intramural competition that in many ways parallels Nova's regular athletic competition.

Nova boasts the first Academic Games Club in the nation, which organizes intramural academic games tournaments at the school. Each year about 45 fourth- and fifth-year level students play a four-week, round-robin Equations tournament. Student gamesters push the parallel with athletics about as far as it will go. Each week complete statistics are compiled giving individual and team won-lost records, total points scored, and league standings. Further, teams carry names like The Mods, Rat Finks, Brain Kids, and Clear Thinkers; each week Nova names "a player of the week."

Altogether there are about 10 leagues at Nova schools, consisting of teams on the elementary and junior and senior high levels. About 70 Nova junior and senior high students annually participate in an all-school tournament built around the Propaganda game on a once-a-week basis for six weeks in November and December. Team and individual champions were crowned during each period and top performers were eligible for Nova's Academic Olympics team.

Early in April, final playoffs are held using Equations,

Propaganda and the Game of Democracy to determine Nova's junior and senior high teams for the Olympics. In 1967, about 100 students participated in the playoffs and 30 were finally selected for the emotion-laden Olympics.

Indeed, the emotional content of the Olympics has been rising steadily along with the stakes. By no means are all schoolmen enthusiastic about the Olympics. What participants actually get out of the national contest is questioned by some critics. They ask whether most games used in the Olympics are sufficiently complex to provide veteran players with a constantly-challenging learning experience. They note that most games yield their structural and instructional mysteries after a few playings. Yet most of the young people appearing at the Nov game site are experienced players who have already mastered the techniques of games.

For most Olympics participants the prime motive spurring play is less avidity for knowledge than thirst for victory. But if the learning pupils acquire from the content can be doubted, the sublimity can't be. Indeed, Robert Allen's Olympics at least seem to have gone a long way towards permitting the apparently brilliant student to bring "glory to the school" in the same way the athlete does.

At the 1967 Academic Olympics, student participants rose to 240 from 140 a year earlier. The students represented eight states—Alabama, Florida, Louisiana, Maine, Mississippi, Pennsylvania, Tennessee and Wisconsin— and competed for the national academic games championship in four different games tournaments.

From the beginning, the players labored under the kleig lights of publicity. Local Florida newspapers, radio and television stations carried the daily results of the tournament. Walter Cronkite's *CBS* 20th Century Program and a National Educational Television program each devoted a good deal of time to the tournament.

After the three-day championships, Olympic participants attended an awards dance where each of the winning schools, and all of the individual winners received trophies. The over-all 1967 champion was Richland High School, of Gibsonia, Pa. To cap the team's honors, the Pennsylvania State Legislature passed a Congratulatory Resolution.

To questions about the tournament's efficacy, Nova gamesters cite the case of Alan Reynolds, a 13-year-old eight grader who finished first among 108 students in the junior division competition in Equations. At the beginning of the 1966-67 school year, however, Alan was at the bottom of his Nova math class and unable to multiply fractions. Nova officials say he was one of the students to benefit from what the school's gamesters call "student interaction generated by the academic games program." Put simply, this means pupils having trouble grasping the concepts involved in a game get individual attention.

Despite Alan's improvement, some Nova educators worry that high-powered competition involving games may lead to an excessive emphasis on winning rather than learning. But whatever the inherent dangers from such contests, the idea has spread to other school systems. A number of school systems are now beginning to experiment with interscholastic competition structured around various games.

For three days each December since 1966, nearly 200 New Orleans high school students have participated in the Mount Carmel Academic Games Tournament, conducted in New Orleans by the Mount Carmel Academy and the Nova Academic Games staff. Competition has been held in Equations, the Propaganda Game and the Game of Democracy. Team and individual champions are awarded prizes by Mount Carmel Academy. In 1967, some of the tournament winners appeared on the television show "Midday." And some of these winners were sent to Fort Lauderdale for the Olympics.

In Pennsylvania's Allegheny County, near Pittsburgh, ten schools constitute what is billed as the first interscholastic Academic Games League in history. The schools first use academic games at the classroom and intramural levels, then select their best students for varsity competition against other schools in the league. The winning teams send representatives to the Nova Olympics.

According to Robert Allen, who helped set up the interscholastic league, the Allegheny program is aimed at "motivating students who have lost interest in a subject, and providing another approach to a subject for students who are having difficulty and inspiring good students by giving them recognition." So far students and teachers seem enthusiastic about the games.

Ralph Stamford, who teaches a seventh grade math class at Turtle Creek Borough School in Allegheny County, is a case in point. He notes that when his students see the signs for exponents and radicals in the Equations game, many of them have already asked their older brothers and sisters what they mean and how to use them in solving problems. "Because these concepts are used in the games, this seventh grade class has already gone over negative exponents, what it means to raise a number to the zero power and lots of other concepts they would not have had in seventh grade class," Stamford says. "In order to be good players they all want to know many different ways of devising an equation to get at the same goal."

At another Allegheny County school, students offered to take double homework to provide additional class time for playing the Propaganda game.

Despite all this enthusiasm, there is much troubling about Allegheny County's—and Nova's—competitive use of games. For one thing, the heavy emphasis often placed on winning may mislead the player as to the real objectives of learning.

That is, the short-term pressures generated for popular success may lead the player to conclude that the ultimate virtue is simply a workable and, at the same time, rather manipulative strategy. So while gaming may produce an academic hero, doubts remain whether the values underpinning his emergence will be any any less superficial than those that have glorified the athlete.

Defenders of games reply that the new-fangled execrises, at their best, seem to be a potent educational innovation because they act on the learning system at so many points. According to Johns Hopkins' Mrs. Boocock, games are useful because they equalize or compensate for differential student status or background and experience.[3] That is, they allow the student to play roles in a large differentiated society of which he ordinarily gets hardly a glimpse. Thus, in the Consumer Game—which involves allocation of income in the face of credit financing, advertising pressures and unpredictable events—pupils must learn something about economics as well as the necessity to defer gratifications. Mrs. Boocock argues that in so doing, players learn intellectual skills relevant for adult roles and, at the same time, certain moral traits, which, she adds, schools usually attempt to inculcate under the general label of "citizenship education."

Equally important, she declares, is that games change the student-teacher relationship, since the exercises, at least in theory, are self-disciplining and self-judging. That is, players must all obey the rules if the game is to continue, and players know whether they have won or lost by their own actions. This, the argument goes, makes students more responsible and autonomous with respect to their own learning and discipline. The teacher, then, is freed to spend more time with individual students.

Finally, Mrs. Boocock claims games raise the level of student motivation and link the school to the world outside by means of the simulated environment. In this Mrs. Boocock's views seem loosely reminiscent of Marshall McLuhan's, at least to the extent that both emphasize the importance of the medium. She notes that games do not directly affect curriculum content, since games can be designed around any content desired. However, she adds that the "underlying principle of the philosophy of educational gaming is that the structure of education may be as important as its content."[4]

At bottom, Johns Hopkins' simulation games are supposed to serve a double function: involve higher proportions of students in classroom activities (since games are a kind of activity which most young people enjoy); and give students some realistic, if vicarious, glimpses of the world outside the school.[5] As a result, they have intrigued educators concerned with how to motivate students considered slow learners or under-achievers.

Most widely used of Johns Hopkins' simulations is Life Career, which, as noted earlier, has been adapted for a spate of different classroom purposes. San Diego schools have used Life Career to acquaint sixth graders with different career possibilities. In 1966, the guidance department of the Palo Alto, Calif., school system added Life Career to its program to help secondary students make more realistic vocational choices. The Pennsylvania Advancement School, a public school in Philadelphia for eighth-grade boys designated as under-achievers, has been experimenting with the game both in the classroom and in intramural competition. (The school is the successor to the now-defunct North Carolina Advancement School.)

In Palo Alto, where the game has been used by Negro and white pupils from varying socio-economic levels, Life Career's use is premised on the notion that many young people simply don't know what criteria to use to make realistic career choices. Thus, Palo Alto's vocational counselors make use of Life Career because the game attempts to imitate or simulate the job, education and marriage market as it exists in American society. At the same time, the game attempts to demonstrate how these markets may affect the life planning of a person, given certain personal characteristics. Life Career has players, rules and a winner.

How does the game work? Players divide into teams of two or three and compete against each other to develop the most "satisfying life" for the next eight to ten years for a hypothetical student—who may be Mary, Mike or George. Here is Mary's profile, presented to players before the game begins:

"Mary is 16 years old and starting her junior year in high school. She is an attractive, small-boned Negro girl with sparkling eyes and vivacious personality.

"Mary's quantitative ability is average and her verbal ability above average. She has done very well in art and music courses she has taken.

"Although neither of Mary's two older sisters have gone to college, both have gone to business school and now have good secretarial jobs. Neither of Mary's parents went to college. Her father is an electronics technician at a local firm earning $6,000 annually. Her mother does not work.

"Mary is debating between a junior college or a four-year state college. She would have to live at home and get a part-time job to help pay expenses. Her parents would like to have her go to college and would help out all they can. Mary does not know what she would like to take and is considering a business course or the dental technician program.

"She has been dating a high school boy who attends another high school. They have become quite serious about one another. However, Jim does not want to go to college, but doesn't know what he would like to do.

"Mary would like to get married and wants to raise a

family, but not immediately. She wants some college before she settles down, but knows she may have difficulty, both academically and financially.

"She has worked Saturdays, holidays and summers at a department store. This has helped provide her clothes and expenses for school."

Given this information about Mary, players begin to make decisions for her by indicating on a decision-sheet how she spends her time from 8 a.m. until 9:30 p.m. Monday through Sunday. The time-span is intended to represent a typical week in one year of Mary's life. During the game, every team plays the same person's life. Although Life Career has many versions, the Palo Alto adaptation of the game is concluded when Mary's life has been planned for ten years by each team playing the game. (Further games can be played by using different profile students.)

In the Palo Alto version, teams receive scores in four areas for each round of the game and a total score at the end of the game itself. The four areas are education, job, family life and leisure. Scores are based on the allocation of time given to each of these areas and are determined by probability data that has been gathered on U.S. Census statistics and other sociological data. Thus, gamesters claim there is accurate information contained within the scoring principles of the exercise.[6]

Here's how scoring works in the education area. When play begins, Mary is just entering her junior year in high school. Teams must first decide what courses she will take. Grades for the courses she takes will determine the education score she gets—and the teams get—for that round. Grades are determined by three factors: a) her ability, b) the number of hours the team has her study for each particular course and c) the roll of the die, which is aimed at introducing subjective variables affecting grades.

Scores in the job area depend on whether a job is a part-time or full-time occupation. If, for example, Mary is old enough to work and does have a part-time job, her score will be decided according to pre-determined formula reflecting family income and the number of hours she may work. The scoring takes into account that some students have more financial need to work; if the need is great, then this students gets a greater number of points for each hour spent on the job.

But once a job becomes a full-time occupation, then job scores are a functon of the job classification and the number of years the profile student has held the job. To students who ask why there is a difference in job scores, game administrators observe that some jobs bring more satisfaction than others. The game presumes that the longer one works at a job, the more satisfaction he may experience.

Then there is scoring having to do with family life. While Mary, say, is unmarried and living at home, or unmarried and going to school, or working, family life scores are based on her personality profile. Here the scoring presumes that some people get more satisfaction out of working around the home than do others. However, once Mary—or one of the other profile students—gets married, this score is a function of her education, the number of years married and the number of children the couple has. Penalties are imposed if there should be a divorce.

Finally, there are scoring provisions that relate to handling of leisure time. During Mary's high school years, her leisure scores are based on the number of hours spent at different leisure activities. Again, the number of points given depends on Mary's personality. While Mary may get more points for each hour spent relaxing with her family, Mike or George may get rewarded for spending time with friends. As is apparent, the scoring is weighted towards results that bring "satisfaction."

Once Mary—or Mike or George—graduates, a leisure-time rating is determined, based on education, family income and marital status. On the basis of this scale, scores are then determined by the number of total hours spent in leisure activities.

The game is usually played in a large room that enables student teams to talk freely among themselves as they make their decisions. Counselors and teachers man four tables: 1) the job table, 2) the education table, 3) the family table, and 4) the scoring table. Palo Alto gamesters explain that built into the exercise is the idea that acquisition of certain things in life requires a certain amount of initiative.

Thus, if a team wants their student—say, Mary—to get a job, they must leave their seats and go to the job table, where they look over the current job market, fill out an application and wait to see whether or not their student gets the job. This, again, is determined by a probability spinner. And if a team wants their student to apply for admission to some school, they must go to the education table, where catalogs are located regarding education alternatives. Once again, they fill out applications for admission and possibly even scholarships.

Finally, if a team wants their student to get married, they must go to the family table where they fill out applications for marriage. Using spinners, the family "counselor" tells the team the age, education and occupational status of their potential spouse. Players then discover that the qualities of the "potential spouse" depends a good deal on the qualities of the hypothetical student whose life they are "playing." If the team wants their student to marry this person, they accept the application and their student is then considered married.

After teams decide on how the average week is spent for that particular year—which is considered one round of the game—players take a summary of the student's schedule to the score table which computes their score for that round of play. At this point they must choose from a series of Unplanned Events cards. These cards introduce into the life of their hypothetical student events that have not been planned for but which may come along in the course of one's life. Once they occur these events must be dealt with in the subsequent planning of their student's life.

As with other games, such as CRISIS and Dangerous Parallel, heavy emphasis is placed on group discussions. However, unlike other games Life Career may be interrupted in mid-play for discussion. This is regarded as an important aspect of the game, since, according to gamesters, it provides for the sharing of ideas regarding decision-making and reinforces learning principles contained in the exercise.

"Students are always encouraged to criticize the game," says one Palo Alto counselor, "since in doing so they are demonstrating their understanding of certain life principles that they may confront in their own lives." Also, counselors caution that the game, while useful, isn't sufficiently strong to carry the full burden of instruction by itself. Thus, discussions and other conventional teaching devices are needed to supplement it.

Palo Alto counselors have used the game in a variety of settings with varying numbers involved. School officials say it has been used most effectively with small groups of students ranging between 10 and 18 in number meeting once a week for one hour. The game has been used in a home economics class of about 20 girls for six consecutive days. Other classroom situations have included a social studies class for several weeks, where additional materials were introduced following the playing of the exercise, and a low-ability English class for a three-week period.[7]

Life Career also has been used in Palo Alto by a group of Project Opportunity students as well as by a group of

Women's Job Corps girls. The game also was used at an all-day symposium for Palo Alto parents, with parents playing the game for a three-hour period followed by about two hours of discussion.

Gamesters note that Life Career provides great flexibility regarding the length of time to spend on it. Ideally, two hours are required at the beginning to get into the game, but each subsequent session with it can be an hour long. Schoolmen warn, however, that playing the game more than two hours at a sitting may end up exhausting players, since they work at it so intensely.

There's no question that pupils get very involved in the game. Gamesters speculate that the fact players are dealing with a human life, even though simulated, has a great deal of appeal for students, who tend to project their own life into that of the profile student with whom they are working. The value of Life Career flows from this great involvement, says Barbara Varenhorst, consulting psychologist for the Palo Alto Unified School District.

Indeed, she says some students have actually decided to postpone marriage or give a child up for adoption as a result of playing Life Career.[8] "This involvement provides the opportunity for teaching some important principles of decision-making and life planning that students have not learned through other methods," says Mrs. Varenhorst. "Putting it more directly, the game requires their attention and involves them emotionally and then they are ready and receptive to learning that we have tried to teach in more rational or didactive methods at other times."

She notes that individuals often dislike practicing decision-making if the consequences are irreversible. Life Career, however, provides decision-making practice in a safe environment. No matter what befalls their profile student, once the game is over the consequences can be left behind and the players as individuals don't have to deal with them personally, says Mrs. Varenhorst. But she claims that pupils do take away from the game increased understanding as a result of the successes and failures they may have made in planning their profile student's life. "Perhaps by this they will not have to personally make the same mistakes," she says.

Equally important, the game exposes students to the practicalities of information-seeking necessary to plan their own lives, say counselors. There's no question that players do in fact learn where to go for a job and school information and how to fill out application blanks.

Finally, says Mrs. Varenhorst, students are confronted with the necessity to declare and define personal values and to establish goals and work out strategies on how to reach these goals. She notes that students have walked away from a session commenting that they had never realized the importance of planning the use of allotted time, or working out a schedule for their life. Said one Palo Alto student: "You really have to plan carefully if you want to work in all the things you want to do in a certain period of time." Another student said she noticed the teams that plan for a life usually end up amassing most of the points by the end of the game.

"It is difficult to help students face these realities through other means," says Mrs. Varenhorst. "It is a necessary part of decision-making and consequently the game is proving to be a great aid in this one area."

A somewhat different use of Life Career—and other games—has been made by the Pennsylvania Advancement School (PAS), a publicly-funded experimental school aimed at dealing with the problems of under-achieving eighth-grade boys. Most of the youngsters have been referred to the school after their own schools have classified them as "under-achievers" and, in some cases, discipline problems.

They come from widely varying socio-economic levels, and

they have greatly differing ability, achievement and attitude levels. They may have behavioral, motivational or remedial problems, or all three. What unites these disparate youngsters is their common alienation from the educational process in their home schools. They are regarded as "misfits" by parents, teachers, counselors, and principals alike.

Basically, what the some 200 pupils at the Advancement School have in common is an inability to perform up to their capacities in a school situation. The mean verbal and non-verbal I.Q.s of the eighth-grade students is usually at or near 100. Yet the reading and arithmetic achievement levels of the boys is usually no more than sixth grade.

What accounts for this alienation? To Dale C. Farran, research associate at the Advancement School, there's no one answer, but she observes "a common feeling of being completely disinterested in the educational process, is the core of the under-achievement problem with which our school must deal."

For these students, time-honored remedial materials don't work, she notes. To attack the under-achiever's unique and common problem, instructional materials must be, according to Mrs. Farran, "interesting, fun and exciting." And, at the same time, they must have educational value that will be meaningful once the students return to their original schools.

Despite reservations about Life Career and other games, Mrs. Farran believes the exercises can deal with three specific aspects of this core problem—lack of involvement—under-achievers share.[9] The first aspect, schoolmen contend, is a lack of the "strategic sense," or ability to know how to attack a problem. That is, the pupils seem to lack the ability to question in directions that will lead to an answer to problems they are facing.

Secondly, under-achieving students are said to have poorly developed ability in "relational" thinking. Advancement

School officials explain that the pupils often find it hard to marshal separate facts or instances into an understandable whole. Mrs. Farran says she can sense in these students "no real feeling of control over their environments—educational, social or psychological." A final aspect of this "core" problem common to under-achievers is an inability to plan systematically. School officials say the pupils find it particularly hard to plan how to move through a specific problem or course of material.

PAS researchers allow that simulations by no means solve all these problems, but they insist that the exercises have helped counter some of the problems of the under-achiever. For one thing, PAS teachers note they often can capitalize on the "halo" effect created by having games in the classroom. The upshot is that students often become involved and are learning and responding before they have quite realized that this is education.[10]

Noting that students learn by experience, Mrs. Farran avers that the value of gaming is that students can put the content of what they are learning into effect immediately. For under-achievers, this is said to be an essential element of the game. "Experience at the Advancement School has indicated that the way to get the students to learn is to make every learning situation an experiential one," says Mrs. Farran.

Especially important in the case of under-achievers is the fact that games serve as a kind of frame of reference, uniting various separate ideas students learned prior to playing the games. That is, the exercises often serve to bring into focus previously-held information that earlier had not been related for these students in any meaningful manner, say PAS researchers.

Mrs. Farran believes games work with under-achievers while other methods fail because they pose a problem within defined boundaries that the students can understand. Also, the students find that games, unlike teachers, parents or friends, are not capricious. They represent to the student an orderly, constant system with which he can cope.[11]

To demonstrate that games can be effective, Mrs. Farran cites the case of a team of four 16-year-old eighth-graders in competition with other teams in the same room playing the Life Career game. They were playing with the profile of a low ability student, and, she recalls, "their first reaction to the whole situation was to treat the game as a joke."

Not surprisingly, midway through the game the team had "planned" its profile into deep troubles—he had quit school, come up with a low paying job, married early and was continually being "blessed" with unplanned children.[12] In fact, observes Mrs. Farran, they had done with their profile much the same things that had happened or were likely to happen to themselves.

Suddenly, the four 16-year-olds became interested in the problem they had created. Noting their profile was falling behind his counterparts as played by other teams in the room, the four players decided to do something about it. They sent the profile back to night school, had him take a second job, and gave him almost no leisure for two years. As a result of these efforts, they managed to "pull him out of it." Says Mrs. Farran: "The excitement and elation that followed is seldom displayed by an under-achiever in a learning situation."

Advancement School researchers point out that games seem to have different effects on under-achievers who come from different socio-economic backgrounds.[13] Games, then, help bring to the surface the values and expectations that different under-achievers unconsciously carry with them. The upshot is that counselors find themselves provided with new insights that enable them to deal more effectively with these troubled youngsters.

Consider the team of middle class players that was given a profile in the Life Career game of a low ability student whose grades were poor. Despite his poor prospects, the team planned a college preparatory program for him in high school. Although the boy's profile described him as disliking studying, the team scheduled for him an inordinate amount of time for studying. When the profile later failed out of college, the team was forced to experiment with other strategies. But teachers recalled they had a hard time doing so because for them the "right" thing for everyone was to go to college.

Students from lower socio-economic backgrounds seem equally committed to rigid life-strategies, although of a different kind. A case in point was provided when a group of 20 poor readers—most of whom were from low socio-economic backgrounds—played Life Career using a high ability profile. Even though the profile's high school grades were excellent, only three of the six teams playing attempted to get the profile a college education.

One of the teams had the profile enter a trade school while the other two had him get a job immediately after graduation from high school. "The students simply were not aware of many of the possibilities that were open to the person presented in the profile," recalls Mrs. Farran. "The teams formulated strategies for this profile on the basis of their own experience."

Advancement School experience with Johns Hopkins' Consumer game provides the same sort of comparison between high and low socio-economic backgrounds. Mrs. Farran explains:[14]

"In the Consumer game, players can borrow money from a bank or a finance company. The best strategy is to borrow from the bank, because its interest rates are lower. Students from middle class backgrounds almost always borrowed from the bank. From the outset of the game, they never considered approaching the finance company. They 'knew,' without knowing why, that the bank was the best place from which to borrow money.

"Students from lower socio-economic backgrounds, however, almost invariably approached the finance company first. They were familiar with finance companies but not with banks. After repeated playings of the game, they began to understand the differences between the two, and turned to the bank."

Counselors believe games can be particularly important for students from lower socio-economic backgrounds because they tend to fill a gap in the youngster's family experience. For most such young people, the thinking and planning incorporated in Life Career, Consumer and other games does not go on in the home. Thus, for these youngsters games may be crucial, since they are likely to provide the only opportunity they will get to plan and think out their lives before having to make irreversible decisions.

Despite the school's success with Life Career, Mrs. Farran retains some reservations about the game. To Mrs. Farran, a game's real purpose is to provide a "sophisticated and satisfactory" outlet for children's expression of primary needs, such as anger, fear, power, need for self esteem and the like. She argues that before games can really convey content, they must enlist children on an emotional level.

Thus, she avers that a really good game is one that combines an outlet for primary needs with some concern for secondary needs, such as problem-solving, decision making, association and other cognitive skills. On the basis of this criteria, Mrs. Farran says the game isn't as good as it could be. For one thing, she notes the game involves no interaction between players competing against each other. Instead, teams play against the pre-determined formulas that are built into the game and provide scores. Competing teams play the game independently; the team with the highest score wins the game.

"Life Career does not meet any primary needs," says Mrs. Farran. "It is geared toward the satisfaction of secondary needs; it is a very cognitive game and to date many of our kids just haven't been interested." On the other hand, she notes that some under-achievers have taken more readily to CRISIS, the Consumer game and a Cornell University-developed exercise called CLUG—for Community Land Use Game. The reason, she says, is that the latter three games do provide players an outlet for primary needs. That is, she adds, these games are satisfying because they require players to make authoritative decisions, wheel and deal and act in a way that is "relevant to their world of the emotions."

But even these games, she cautions, are subject to abuse. In fact, she warns that "escalating competition" into elaborate intramural and interscholastic leagues may actually be harmful in that they place emphasis on winning and distract from the original purpose of games. At least to Mrs. Farran, games aren't ends in themselves, but devices to get reluctant youngsters involved in seemingly dry course material content. And at the same time, to spur pupils to "push beyond the boundaries of the classroom and make what goes on inside the class part of their everyday thinking," she says.

Toward this end, she thinks it may be useful for children to produce their own games. The suggestion is by no means frivolous. Other schoolmen, among them Cleo Cherryholmes, professor of political science at Michigan State University, suggest that games might have greater value if students built and tested the simulations by themselves. In this way, the argument goes, students would derive additional insights into the game's structure, and, therefore, the social process simulated.

The possibility that game design may one day be a routine

classroom assignment raises a basic question: How does one make a game? Although several social scientists are developing a theory of design, there are at present few guidelines on just what elements should go into a game. Johns Hopkins' Sarane Boocock has observed, "Game design is not only not a science, it is hardly a craft, but rather an 'art' in the sense that we have no explicit rules to transmit."

In the absence of firm rules, the Foreign Policy Association has suggested some of the elements that might go into a simulation game:[15]

First, the exercise must entail an objective that the teacher—or student—thinks he wants to learn or teach. For example, the objective may be to teach some concept, such as "balance of power," or to acquaint participants with the difficulties of decision making.

Second, the designer must construct a simplified model—or "dramatization"—of the process or system that will best serve the objectives.

Third, the designer must spell out the various actors or teams required to demonstrate the effectiveness of the model. Games range from two participants (the Family game) to 30 or more (Dangerous Parallel or INS).

Fourth, the players must have resources (troops, money, votes, etc.) to exchange in competition with other players. Frequently, precise values are given resources so that success or failure can be evaluated after the game.

Fifth, as the players go about trading resources they must have some clear objective or goal. That is, they must be seeking reelection, an improved lot in life, resolution of an international conflict or some other goal.

Sixth, there must be limits or rules set on what is permissible behavior. Also, time limits must be determined for the various stages of play. Whether the rules are elaborate and strict, or loose and simple will depend on the objectives of the game.

Finally, some games, such as Dangerous Parallel, begin with a "scenario" that sets the stage and instructs the participants for the beginning of play. The scenario also will describe the various players, their objectives and resources, and the rules by which they must be governed.

Simulations are often far more subtle—and sophisticated—than they at first appear. To design a successful social simulation, a great deal of ingenuity is required, as can be seen from looking at Johns Hopkins' efforts. By its very definition, a social simulation is concerned primarily with that part of individuals' environment that consists of other people, groups and organizations. The chief question here for the designer is how to incorporate the environment into the game's structure.

According to Hopkins' James Coleman, there are ordinarily two solutions, either or both of which are used in any specific game. Writes Coleman:[16]

"One is to let each player in the game act as a portion of the social environment of each other player. The rules of the game establish the obligations upon each role, and the players, each acting within the rules governing his role, interact with one another. The resulting configuration constitutes a social subsystem, and each player's environment consists of that subsystem, excluding himself." (An example is the legislature portion of Hopkins' Democracy game, which consists of players in a single subsystem. Each player is a legislator, and interactions are with other players in their role as legislators.)

Coleman adds that "A second way in which the social environment is embodied in a social simulation game is in the rules themselves. The rules may contain contingent responses of the environment, representing the actions of persons who are not players, but nevertheless relevant to the individual's action. A game using this solution can in fact be a one-player game, in which the whole of this player's environment represented by the game is incorporated in the rules."

A case in point is the Life Career game, which may involve only one player making decisions about a hypothetical student. Responses to the player's decisions occur through the environmental response rules, which represent responses of: teachers in school, school admissions officers, potential employers, and potential marriage partners. However, none of these roles is represented by a player in the game. Instead, the probable responses of persons in such roles to various actions of the player are embodied in the environmental response rules. The actual responses are determined by these rules in conjunction with a chance mechanism. The player in the Life Career game, which may or may not be computerized, plays for a score, and the only relation to other players is through a comparison of scores.

Most games use a combination of these two solutions. Part of the environment is represented by other players, and part by the environmental response rules. Importantly, the social simulation's many rules often reflect the assumptions about behavior on which the simulation is based.

As Coleman observes, each game designed as a social simulation implies a quite specific theory about behavior in the area of life being simulated. He notes these theoretical elements are mirrored primarily in the game's goal-specification rules—which spell out what the player's goal is and how it is to be reached. But these assumptions also may form part of the game's procedures and environmental response rules.

Coleman points out there are close affinities between games and one type of behavior theory: [17]

"Whether the competing unit is an individual or a team, the

game functions because each individual pursues his own goal. Thus a social simulation game must necessarily begin with a set of individuals carrying out purposive behavior toward a goal. It is hardly conceivable, then, that the theoretical framework implied by a social simulation game be anything other than a purposive behavior theory.

"This means a definite theoretical stance on several issues: On the issue in social theory of expressing the assumptions of the theory at the level of the individual or at the level of the collectivity or social system, the use of games implies taking the former, individualist position. On the issue of purposive theory vs. positivist theory (where behavior is described as a lawful response to an environmental stimulus), the use of games implies the purposive orientation.

"On the issue of purposive, goal-oriented behavior vs. expressive theory (where the individual act is an expression of some inner tension without regard to a goal), the use of games again implies the purposive orientation. On the issue of behavior determined by personality or other historical causes not currently present vs. behavior determined by the constraints and demands of the present (and possibly expected future) situation, the use of games implies the latter, the theory of present and future-governed behavior.

"On the issue of purposive, goal-oriented behavior vs. behavior governed wholly by normative expectations and obligations (as, for example, occurs in some organization theory, where the individual's interest plays no role, and he is predicted to behave simply in accord with organizational rules), the use of games implies the former, goal-oriented position."

To sum up, the use of games takes as its starting point—except in those cases where the competing unit is a team—the self-interested individual, and requires that any non-self-interested behavior emerge from pursuit of his goals, as means to individual ends. For this reason, Coleman cautions that social simulations using a collectivity, such as a family, as a team to form a competing unit, are not as theoretically complete as are those games in which the individual player is the competing unit.

Be that as it may, it's likely that in the future more attention will be devoted to the social theory underpinning simulations, since this is one of the potentially controversial aspects of games. So far the tendency has been to take for granted the validity of the assumptions on which games are based. They probably will get closer scrutiny in the future.

It's obvious, however, that games are by no means simple affairs, and it's hard to understand the decision of a Midwest high school in 1966 to turn down a proposal to use in its history classes a politico-military game, called Diplomacy, on the grounds that it was "simply entertainment." Games are more than entertainment. But whether games are all they are claimed to be is something that will be considered in the last chapter. Meantime, games are penetrating nearly every level of education, including the elementary.

Chapter 6

SIXTH GRADERS AND SUMERIA

"... whenever we try to trace the origin of a skill or a practice which played a crucial role in the ascent of man, we usually reach the realm of play."—*Eric Hoffer*

Contemptuous of change, the average American classroom, whether ghetto or middle class, betrays few traces of the revolution said to be sweeping American education. With its emphasis on memorization of facts and internal control of students, the average classroom remains, at best, bland, and, at worst, deadly dull. Nonetheless, stirrings are underway in some sectors of education.

Even while little apparent in most schools, a few drastic changes have been introduced into the educational system. Teaching machines, team teaching, autotelic learning and strategy games are but a few of the innovations currently being tested in the small but growing number of schools receptive to experimentation. Despite the fancy gadgetry sometimes employed, these changes reflect far more than the encroachment of technology into the classroom. Indeed, they suggest recent shifts in the substance of educational theory itself. For example, Jerome Bruner claims:[1]

"More than ever before, we are concerned with the nature of the educational process, with the goals of education, with the impact of change—and besides with the techniques and devices that can be used in improving the educational enterprise. There has been much inventiveness . . . Indeed to the outside observer it must seem as if we were prepared to embark upon a permanent revolution in education. And I think we are entering such a period."

To the extent that such a revolution is taking place, educators like Bruner and Jean Piaget, the French psychologist, must be given a good deal of the credit. Both have emphasized the development of instructional theories based on the various stages of a youngster's intellectual development. Put simply, the educators argue for teaching methods geared less to classroom order than to the actualities of how children learn.

For the disciples of Piaget and Bruner, students are not to be perceived as the passive recipients of facts to be regurgitated later. Instead, the focus is on the young person's total response to his environment; his time in the classroom is viewed as but one aspect of his overall development. Consequently, educators influenced by Piaget and Bruner have called for teaching techniques that dovetail with the child's broader intellectual and emotional development.

Viewing learning as a process that goes on in and out of the classroom, both Piaget and Bruner have stressed the importance of the "play element" in child development. Bruner declares that "observations of young children and of the young of other species suggest that a good deal of their play must be understood as practice in coping with the environment."[2] As a result, Bruner and others have advocated the use of strategy games in the classroom to tap this source of learning motivation.

In his 1965 essay, "Man: A Course of Study," Bruner called for a social studies curriculum for elementary students that would emphasize man—"his nature as a species, the forces that shaped and continue to shape his humanity." Throughout the curriculum three questions would recur: "What is human about human beings. How did they get that way? How can they be made more so?"[3]

Bruner called for development of teaching techniques that would pose the three questions directly to the children, so that their own views could be brought into the open and so that they could establish some points of view of their own. "We seek exercises and materials through which our pupils can learn wherein man is distinctive in his adaptation to the world, and wherein there is discernible continuity between him and his animal forbears," says Bruner.

To effectively pursue the three questions, Bruner suggested exploration of five areas closely associated with the evolution of man and his distinctiveness as a species. These great humanizing forces cited were tool-making, language, social organization, the management of man's prolonged childhood, and man's urge to explain.

Of these five areas, the teaching of social organization particularly lends itself to use of strategy games, according to Bruner. The Harvard educator believes that the exercises can bring social organization into the personal consciousness of children. Specifically, he believes they can help make children aware that there is a structure in a society and that this structure isn't fixed once and for all. As a result of playing certain newly-developed games, he avers children will see that society is an integrated pattern and that you cannot change one part of the pattern without other parts of the society changing with it. Says Bruner:[4]

"Games go a long way toward getting children involved in understanding language, social organization, and the rest; they also introduce, as we have already noted, the idea of a theory of these phenomena. We do not know to what extent these games will be successful, but we shall give them a careful try. They provide a superb means of getting children to participate actively in the process of learning—as players rather than spectators."

The upshot of the Bruner-Piaget theories is that strategy games are no longer confined to universities and secondary schools; they have spread into elementary levels. One group currently at work to translate Bruner's views into an actual curriculum for fifth graders is Education Development Center Inc. (formerly Educational Services Inc.), a nonprofit Cambridge, Mass.-based outfit funded by foundation grants to innovate educational programs. Already the center's Elementary Social Studies Program has developed and packaged for distribution to grade schools a one-year curriculum—entitled Man: A Course of Study—based on Bruner's essay.

Using audio-visual techniques, films and other new-fangled devices, the course initially confronts children with opportunities to observe the lives of other animals—such as baboons, salmon and the herring gull—in ways that will help them think concretely about what it means to be a human being. Later, the unit turns to a three-fold analysis of human culture: ecological adaptation, social structure and man's overpowering urge to explain and to believe.

To teach these areas of human experience, the unit focuses on the little-known culture of the Netsilik Eskimos, inhabitants of the Arctic tundra in Canada's Northwest Territories. Through study of the Netsilik, "we hope to illuminate for children both the infinite variety and the commonality of human experience," says Peter Dow, director of the EDC's Social Studies Curriculum Program.

According to Dow, by studying simple human societies in elementary school, teachers can expose children early to the important process of man's ecological adaptation; that is, the adaptation of man to his physical environment. Thus, the Cambridge educators selected the Netsilik Eskimos because they illustrate how man's culture can be shaped by his physical environmnt. In the course, fifth graders study how this remote human group has fashioned a viable material culture out of a paucity of resources: rocks, snow and the bodies of animals.

To illustrate how Netsilik society made use of a primitive

technology in comparatively recent times, the center has included in its curriculum package a game called "Caribou Hunting with Bow and Arrow." As Dow explains, the game is aimed at teaching a multiplicity of points about Netsilik social organization and technology:[5]

"How does a hungry Eskimo employ his human and material resources to intercept a nice fat caribou? We have already identified the material elements of Netsilik caribou hunting technology: kayak, spear, bow and arrow, inukshuks (piles of stone that look like men to caribou). To this we add the human resources of hunters and beaters. On a game board designed to simulate an actual Eskimo hunting area, children manipulate these resources in a way that results in a successful caribou kill. As they devise alternative hunting strategies students perceive that it is through careful organization of technological and human resources that man is able to master his physical environment.

"This leads us to a closer look at the social structure of the caribou camp. Who hunts with whom? How are the roles of hunters and beaters determined? What supporting activities occupy the women while the men hunt? At this time of year the characteristic social unit is the extended family. Often two brothers will hunt together with their sons or other relatives. The catch is shared informally throughout the group. A precise division of labor exists: men hunt, and women butcher the catch and prepare the skins for tents and clothing. Within the harmonious balance that exists between technological requirements and social norms there is considerable flexibility; different numbers of hunters and beaters are used, and even different methods, and despite the sharing, intense competition prevails. This interrelationship between specialization and flexibility of alternatives is a fundamental component of human cultural adaptation which teachers can apply to their discussions of many other societies."

How does the game work? Simulating bow-and-arrow hunters, groups of three children play the game around a desk-sized map that represents 10 square miles near Pelly Bay—the actual area in the Northwest Territories where the Netsilik still live. In the game, two eskimo players intercept a "herd" of caribou moved by a third player during a "fall migration."

As the game begins, a herd of 40 caribou—whose movements are represented by a pair of dice—appear at the top of the board at a large dot. The herd migrates to the south during the game. The herd is moved by the third player—known as the Caribou Player—who marks the herd's route with green arrows.

The Caribou Player's main job is to roll two six-sided dice. The herd moves in the direction indicated by the combined letters on the upper faces of the two dice. Thus, one die indicating S and the other die indicating E would mean that the herd moves Southeast. However, one die indicating W and the other die showing a blank face means that the herd moves West. If both dice show blank faces, the herd remains still and "grazes."

The herd always moves three dots in a straight line on each turn; these moves are represented by a green arrow on the game board, or map. As for the hunters, they would like to know exactly where the herd will go. In fact, all they know is that it will move south as it migrates.

After each caribou move, each hunter may move one dot in any direction he wishes. Or he can opt to remain in the same place if he wants. Each of the two hunters marks his route with red arrows as he tries to get close to the herd. Importantly, the hunters do not move according to the roll of the dice; they plan their moves.

A kill is automatic if a hunter moves to a dot adjacent to the herd, or if the herd moves onto a dot adjacent to him.

The game presupposes that a hunter cannot shoot accurately at a distance of greater than one dot.

The game, however, does not end when a caribou is killed; the rest of the herd flees. Once the herd is attacked, it flees five dots in the opposite direction without completing its move. An important factor for the hunters to consider in the game is the wind, which always blows out of the east. The game realistically takes into account that caribou can smell much better than they can see.

In the game, the caribou herd can see a man one dot away, but it can smell a man who is upwind two dots away. Man's scent is carried by the wind from east to west; in fact, a plastic Scent Indicator shows the area where the herd can smell the man. The hunter's task is to develop a strategy that will enable him to get close to the herd without being seen or sniffed first. The game continues until the migrating herd reaches the edge of the board.

Afterwards, players in post-game sessions discuss what strategies were most successful; the youngsters are asked to mull some of the difficulties in bow and arrow hunting. Considering that the caribou season is four weeks long, the players are asked to ponder whether hunters could be provided with enough skins for their families by hunting with the bow.

The author can attest that bagging a caribou is no easy trick. In a play of the game in one of EDC's modest game rooms, the author and a hunting companion set out after a great caribou herd. Unhappily, the two huntsmen made a basic mistake right off: they hunted together rather than splitting up. This minimized chances of felling a caribou, since the map is simply too large for a pair of hunters to stay together and still be successful.

The result: Both hunters would have gone hungry for the 24-hour period simulated by one play of the game.

This isn't the only "Caribou Hunting" game offered by the Cambridge gamesters. Another version of the same game involves several additional players, some of whom act as beaters driving the caribou into specifically-prepared traps where their fellow huntsmen wait with spears.

What do children really learn from such games? One result, hopes Dow, is that students will "explore the intriguing fact that survival is a common concern for all living organisms, including man, and that the mechanisms for insuring survival and continuity of life are extremely numerous and diverse." To learn this, he avers youngsters will realize that a certain amount of cooperation and sharing is essential for the survival of a society, just as it is for the Netsilik.

To further emphasize these survival laws, EDC gamesters have developed—with the help of Abt Associates—a second Eskimo game, "Seal Hunting." Background of the game is the coming of winter, which each year deeply affects the lives of the Netsilik. With the caribou herds gone, the Eskimos trek out onto the sea ice where they build their winter camp and hunt seals through breathing holes.

Cambridge game-makers note that cooperation and group solidarity is crucial during the severe winter months when temperatures reach 50 degrees below zero and seals provide the only sustenance. "Under these conditions group structure, social behavior and religious beliefs become the focus of our concern," says Dow. At this critical time of the year, he notes, only the clever deployment of human resources, plus a bit of luck or the seeming intervention of sea spirits, can make the difference between survival and starvation. Observes Dow:[6]

"Seal-hunting in midwinter is a cooperative enterprise. Seals keep open as many as 20 widely scattered breathing holes which are difficult to find when snow is deep on the ice.

Thus there are advantages in large group hunting, which allows a number of holes to be watched at once. A solitary hunter may be able to feed his family for a month or two, but . . . statistics reveal that cooperative hunting partnerships, accompanied by rigid meat-sharing practices, provide the best protection against the threat of starvation.

"Children grasp these facts quickly when they play a seal-hunting game programmed so that the hunter has a one-in-six chance of catching a seal, a realistic statistical probability for the Eskimos. Each seal provides a hunter with a seven-day food supply. Some hunters may have good luck, but it is soon clear that others starve unless the catch is shared. The students are free to devise their own solutions, and some reveal the nurturing of a capitalistic society. With this experience they can assess the significance of the sharing patterns and the social relationships that organize the Netsilik midwinter camp."

In short, the game stimulates a group hunt, and provides an opportunity for children to discover the importance of group sharing and to test out different hunting strategies, say gamesters.

For a class of 30 children, the teacher should provide five "Seal Hunting" game boards. In the game, six children gather around a single board, each of which has 168 removable plastic corks. The boards represent the ice of Pelly Bay and each cork represents a breathing hole of a seal. The players try to catch a seal by selecting one breathing hole each turn for 20 turns, representing 20 days of hunting.

When a hunter finds a paper seal under his overturned cork, he is considered successful. Importantly, each seal caught is worth seven days of food supply. Of the game's six players, five are Eskimo hunters. The sixth is a referee who keeps score for the game. Object of the game—which involves several variations during three class periods—is to let children experiment with hunting and sharing strategies that solve the problem of an unpredictable food supply.

Before play begins, children are given a chance to examine the board and notice how it works. By removing the rubber bands and turning over the top portion, they will see that the board consists of holes arranged in 24 circled "ranges," each representing the area of one seal's breathing holes. At this point the class discusses questions like: What does an Eskimo hunter know about seals that can help him hunt?

The game is quite simple, although it does involve a macabre grisliness. The exercise begins after a referee opens the game board and places one Seal Sticker in a hole in each of the 24 seal ranges. The referee records the players' names on a record chart, and distributes a strip of four labels to each player. Each hunter then chooses a hole and "hunts."

If a hunter finds a seal, he places the first label in a column under his name on the record chart. If he doesn't find a seal, the player places a label from his pre-game supply in his column for that simulated day. The same steps are repeated for 20 "days." Then the referee with what seems to be an arresting combination of fairy tale whimsy and Al Capone realism, tallies the total number of seals caught, hungry days and "dead" hunters in the appropriate boxes on the record chart.

At least theoretically, the game is supposed to generate a good deal of tension. After a hunter has had three consecutive "hungry days," he is considered too weak to hunt and must rely on food supplies of others, if, that is, others can be presuaded to help. A hunter who goes hungry for five consecutive days is "dead," and out of the game.

In post-game sessions, players are asked to consider what ways could be devised to assure fewer hungry days for the whole group. In this way, gamesters hope the players will discover for themselves the necessity for some kind of sharing as well as the need for some kind of remembering system. That is, a system in which players can keep tabs jointly on which holes have been tried and which ones haven't been tried.

In second and third plays of the game, it is understood players are expected to try to reduce the number of hunters who "die." They are reminded that the purpose of the game, according to instruction materials, is "to see which group can survive with the fewest hungry days." This spurs players to look for new techniques for catching seals. Frequently, gamesters assert, players find that if they cooperate by hunting near each other on the sea ice, they may cover the territory of one seal, thus increasing their chances of getting at least one a day and minimizing the possibility of getting none on several consecutive days.

At the end of the third class period, such questions as the following are put to the fifth graders: "In what ways is this game like real seal hunting? On what does success depend in this game? If you were an Eskimo seal hunter, would you prefer to live alone, with your extended family, or in a large group? Why?"

The sprinkling of elementary schools now beginning to make use of the EDC-distributed games are by no means alone. Not only are other elementary schools experimenting with games, but some recently-developed exercises greatly exceed in complexity the relatively simple non-computer games assembled in Cambridge.

Take the spate of economic games produced at the Board of Cooperative Educational Services (BOCES) in Northern Westchester County, N.Y., where researchers have been turning out computer-based games aimed at teaching sixth graders the principles of economics. Under grants from the U.S. Office of Education, such exercises have been devised as the Sumerian Game, concerned with the economics of an ancient civilization; Sierra Leone, aimed at teaching the conomics of an underdeveloped country; and Free Enterprise, which puts the student in charge of a toy store and later a toy factory to give him simulated experience with economic problems that occur in these occupations.

Of these exercises the most widely-used and complex is the Sumerian Game, which, incidentally, involves some 16,000 lines of instructions to the computer. Yet BOCES gamesters claim that sixth graders have no difficulty playing the game, which was invented in 1962 by Bruse Moncreiff of the IBM Corp. and later revised by Mabel Addis.

Basically, the game is designed to teach sixth graders some principles of economics as they applied to the neolithic revolution in Mesopotamia during the fourth millennium B.C. After an introductory programmed tape and slide presentation, the pupil seats himself at a computer terminal and assumes the role of Luduga I, priest-king of Lagash in the year 3,500 B.C.

The player is then presented with a series of problematic situations and must indicate on the typewriter his decisions concerning such questions as how much grain to plant for the year, how much to save, and how much to feed the people.[7] As the game progresses, the pupil is faced with problems of expanding population, irrigation, foreign trade and other complex situations which confront a changing economy.

Spicing the game at intervals are technological innovations and randomly-introduced disasters. For each of the "rulers's" decisions the computer responds appropriately, causing the economic development of the country to proceed in a way which is dependent on the wisdom of the pupil's decisions.

Here is the inventor's description of how the game works:[8]

"The general situation is presented to the student by a narrative with pictorials. The idea of an agricultural cycle of planting and harvesting is introduced. The initial problem of how much grain to set aside for the next planting is posed. The student, by trial and error, will arrive at a satisfactory figure, which must correspond to the rate-of-return parameter built into the model. Each time the student enters a 'planting' figure, the model computes a 'food-supply' position at the end of the following harvest.

"A constant planting figure that adequately feeds the people will not stabilize the model, since the population will tend to grow. The young priest-king must alter his estimates. Within the limits of the technology of the times, grain can be stored only for relatively short periods. Rotting and destruction by rodents will take place. But there are natural and man-made catastrophes which must be prepared for by some storage of grain. These catastropies are introduced in the form of floods, storms, field and granary fires, etc. The student soon learns how much surplus to provide in order to minimize human suffering and waste due to grain spoilage simultaneously."

The student runs into further troubles as the game proceeds. Initially, the player discovers that increasing amounts of grain to be saved for seeding appear to stabilize the model at an acceptable nourishment level. But this insight doesn't serve him in all cases.

For one thing, the return on an increasing number of seeds planted in the same land area does not increase linearly. In fact, the return drops close to zero when seeds are planted so close that few plants can mature. Consequently, more land must be tilled. This gives the player an opportunity to order public works projects, such as the construction of irrigation ditches.

In the course of playing, students find that while workers removed from primary food production affect the temporary food supply, the work they do tends to increase food production in the long run. The model is so constructed that widespread starvation is the result of a late decision to increase the acreage.

At the same time, the effects of undernourishment are felt not only as a decrease in the population, but also as a lingering lowering of the production per man. One or more such periods of starvation may so lower the vitality of the civilization it can no longer survive. Says Moncreiff:[9]

"If the student and his city-state survive these early crises, it is possible to begin building a small surplus. This can, of course, never become extensive until technological developments allow the storage of energy in a form less corruptible than that of grain. If a high level of nutrition is achieved over a substantial number of years, such technological innovations will be favored. There are other factors involved in the rate of technological developments, such as the number of people involved in the related art or craft. Our priest-king is given the opportunity to allocate people and resources to various techniques known to exist at that period in Sumer. If he does so, and also is able to maintain a stable food supply, several inventions will be reported to him at random times, which he in turn can use or not as he sees fit. The utilization of many of these inventions will provide ways of 'capitalizing' currently available energy in the creation of goods which can then be substituted for scarce energy in time of crisis. This is perhaps the major lesson to be learned from this exercise, and the model should be constructed in such a way as to make this point clear.

"Other possible activities for simulation in the game are the organization of social groups in Lagash, the city-state, and trade with neighboring states. . . .

"In summary, the objective of the game is to make decisions in such a way that the city-state survives a series of natural and political crises, that the population grows, and that a high rate of technological innovation is maintained. These goals are numerous, diffuse and possibly conflicting, compared with typical parlor games."

During the game, the student plays through the reigns of several priest-kings, the first of which is Luduga I. The youngster plays the game by himself, sitting at typewriter terminal controlled by the computer. The computer poses problems and the student responds by punching out answers on the typewriter terminal.

The game begins after the rules and initial economic conditions of Lagash have been given the child by the computer. After assuming the role of the priest-king, the player is presented with his first problematic situation: "We have harvested 5,000 bushels of grain to take care of 500 people. How much of this grain shall be set aside for the next season's planting, and how much will be stored in the warehouse? The remainder will be given to the people to eat." This problem is repeated throughout the entire game; each harvest represents six months in the life of a ruler.

Throughout the exercise the child makes decisions and enters his answers at the computer terminal. The computer immediately returns a progress report, including the number of bushels of grain in the harvest reaped from the seed grain set aside for planting, a report on his inventory, crop losses from disaster, and the size of the population.[10]

As noted earlier, the game gets tougher as it goes along. The rule of the first Luduga is devoted to the solution of problems pertaining to an agricultural economy. In the game's second phase, the player attempts to apply his surplus grain to the development of crafts. Finally, he is introduced to trade and the more complex problems that confront a changing economy. "The rate and trend of the development will depend on the wisdom of the child's decisions," says one BOCES researcher.

How good is the Sumerian Game? Very good, insists Richard Wing, coordinator of the Curriculum Research Center of BOCES. But on the basis of a recent experiment, he concedes "we have not demonstrated that our games are more effective in teaching economic concepts" than conventional methods. Still, he notes the study "demonstrated that the games took less time (to teach the concepts) than the classroom method used in comparison."

Even though there is little evidence as to the amount of learning that takes place during the game, Wing believes the "students are learning some principles of economics and some facts about ancient Sumer." At the same time, he declares the game enables the teacher to individualize and tailor instruction for students progressing at different rates. Says Wing: "The Sumerian Game fulfills three of the conditions of variability set up as criteria for learning environments likely to aid in individualizing instruction: independenc in rate of progress, variability in kind of sequence, and capability to provide appropriate responses." [11]

As the San Anselmo experience discussed in chapter three suggests, the making of games isn't limited to major research centers like those in Cambridge and Northern Westchester County. Indeed, the growing popularity of games has spurred a number of individual teachers to devise their own simulations. In some cases the results have been provocative; a few such home-made exercises have dealt more directly with civil rights and other sensitive issues than some of the more established games.

An example is Disunia, developed a couple of years ago by David Yount and Paul DeKock, history teachers at El Capitan High School in Lakeside, Calif. The two men, who team teach U.S. history to eleventh graders, decided to consider games after tiring of wrestling with bored and uninterested students. "We wondered whether our problem had been inherent in our approach: when we *stand over* our classes and teach history (rather than *sit among* students *learning* history), aren't we trying to teach democratic principles in an authoritarian manner?" wondered Messrs. Yount and DeKock.[12]

The result of this questioning was Disunia, which is aimed at allowing students as much freedom from domination by the teacher as possible. To begin the history game the classroom is organized into action areas and the usual desks are replaced with chairs and tables.

In the game, each of the course's roughly 70 students becomes a member of one of 13 colonies which has been established on the planet Edonia (i.e., the classroom), by refugees fleeing an atomic holocaust which had enveloped the earth. The refugees call their new nation Disunia, since the game is based on the jealousies having to do with colony sovereignity. Seeking to simulate the frustrations faced by Americans during the crisis of 1781-1789, the game roughly parallels the Articles of Confederation period.

One principle on which the game is based is competition, built into the exercise by a reward and penalty system devised by the two teachers:[13]

"Reward comes immediately from accumulated points representing power directly useful in the education game, rather than from letter grades useful mainly as instruments to mollify parents and teachers. To accomplish this type of competition and reward, simulations require various types of point systems. In Disunia we set up a 'money' system consisting of mimeographed CGS's (Consumer Goods and Services) bills. We awarded this play money to students for performing specific tasks which we integrated into the simulation.

"The CGS's we divided into two categories: Blue, which represented 'industrial' wealth; and Green, represented 'agricultural' wealth. Each group was designated as primarily an industrial or agricultural colony; hence, an individual in an industrial colony was 'paid' in Blue CGS's; an individual in an agricultural, in Green. Students were told that the object was to have their colonies reach a favorable balance between Blue and Green CGS's by the end of each playing period and that part of their reward (i.e., grade for the unit) would depend on how well their group accomplished this objective. Therefore, in Disunia, a student worked not only for himself but also for his group."

According to Yount and DeKoch, such competition leads to deeper involvement on the part of students in written course material. Indeed, the teachers claim that some students were more willing to read books like *The Federalist Papers,* since the knowledge used from such reading could be used in the game. "By thus using knowledge as power in their lives, these able students no longer though of historical knowledge as a dead thing embalmed on paper which would only interest a teacher," say Young and DeKock.

In addition to competition and decision-making, the game also provides an opportunity for *commitment* — what the teachers describe as the "time and place for students to act on the basis of strong feelings about a decision they have made." What provides this opportunity is that part of the game in which student-colonizers devise their own constitution, which they may accept or reject during a vote.

While the constitution is being debated in a specially-convened assembly, a "pressure factor" is introduced into the game by the administrator. This is the newly-announced fact that three of the colonies have succeeded in capturing and taming certain man-like creatures—the Appletans—and have integrated them into their economies as slaves.

Predictably, this disrupts delegates at the constitutional convention, since they can't agree on how the Appletans should be represented in Disunia. In one recent play of the game, heated arguments developed over whether these creatures were really people. A dozen students made impassioned speeches from the convention floor for the abolition of slavery; an equal number argued that each colony should have the right to make up its own mind on the issue.

The convention dissolved into chaos when several colonies walked out of the assembly to form their own slave-free nation, which they decided to call Potentiana. Setting themselves up in an adjoining room, the dissident students reacted angrily when a teacher entered the room to keep order. "We're capable of ruling ourselves," one student told the teacher. After the teacher left, the Potentianians elected a leader and took steps to use their economic power to try to force Disunia into agreeing to "a fairer treatment of the Appletans, who are just as human as you are," as one rebellious student put it.

Meanwhile, back at the convention, rabble-rousers began crying for war, which was allowed in the game even though it was extremely costly to a colony's wealth. After one and one-half days of debate, one intellectual girl suddenly had had enough. Speaking into a microphone, she declared: "You fathead boys yelling for war don't realize what it'll cost us." Later, saner voices prevailed and a summit conference was arranged between the two nations during a lunch break.[14]

It wasn't long before the Potentianians decided to move away from their original absolutist position. Unfortunately for them, the 13 colonies' economies were so interwoven that they could not survive independently. As a result, they were forced to compromise, even though a few players were sufficiently committed to their position to take an "F" group grade (which they would have received had their colony failed economically). The constitution was saved when it was agreed upon to have all the colonies contribute an equal sum for the purchase of the freedom and education of the Appletans.

The question remains, however, whether the game generates as much light as heat. Messrs. Yount and DeKock allow the evidence is ambiguous, but they nevertheless insist the experience is valuable:[15]

"On multiple choice tests on knowledge of the year 1781, students showed no significant increase over students taught in the traditional lecture-discussion methods we had used in the past. However, in essay tests and in comments to their teachers, students at various ability levels showed understanding of concepts not usually understood by high school history students: how men set in motion forces over which they lose control; how change is inevitable; how important historical change is often shaped by those who have the least to lose; how men get imprisioned by ideas and emotions and how they're willing to sacrifice everything for them; and how dramatically parallel Disunia proved to be with *The Lord of the Flies*, a novel many of the students have read."

Whatever the merits of Disunia, it's one of a fledgling number of games that attempt to deal in one form or another with the burning issues of the day. One game that approaches the civil rights question in a rather more indirect way is the Game of Empire, one version of which is now being distributed to junior high school history teachers by the Education Development Center.

The game deals with mercantilism and trade regulations in the 18th-century British Empire. In "Empire" six teams represent competing interest groups — merchants, Virginia planters, etc. — that buy and sell cargoes shipped all over the world. Winner of the week-long game is the student with the most successful voyages, which are fraught with peril since ships can sink or shippers can get caught as smugglers (vagaries determined by the spin of a wheel).

Some teachers have objected to the game on grounds it seems to teach and encourage immoral behavior, such as bribing, smuggling and slave trading. Game-makers answer that slavery, bribery and smuggling were integral parts of 18th century trading and, therefore, should be allowed in the game.

Nonetheless, questions as to the morality of slavery are not automaically raised by playing "Empire." Unless the teacher makes a deliberate effort after the game, the opportunity to discuss the matter will simply be lost. "It is hard to over-emphasize the importance of a 'de-briefing' or discussion session after the game has been played," says Peter Wolff, editorial director of the EDC's Social Studies Curriculum Program. "Without such discussions, much of the value of 'Empire' will be lost."

For a time, the Cambridge gamesters considered a "slave" game as a supplement to "Empire." The idea of the game was to confront students with the moral problems of slave trade; this would be done by devising an exercise that would familiarize them with the horrors of the middle passage. But the idea was dropped. Explains Wolff:[16]

"On reflection, however, we decided that this was probably damaging to the children, especially Negro children. Not only was the game fatally rigged (the closest a player could come to 'winning' was merely to survive through several rounds of playing ending up as a slave), so that no child could experience any real pleasure of winning, but it also seemed that playing the game could contribute to a low self-estimate by Negro children. The game was never tried out, therefore; we felt that the moral problems of slave trade could better be dealt with in some other, non-game fashion."

For the most part, games devised for secondary and elementary schools have been aimed at the long-neglected areas of social studies and economics. But the proliferation of strategy games has been so great that it's easy to overlook recently-contrived exercises aimed at teaching adolescents the principles of business and geography.

Consider the eight-game series developed for high school social studies and business classes by Erwin Rausch, vice president, manufacturing, of the Wing Co., a division of Aero-Flow Dynamics, Inc. The exercises are now being distributed to secondary schools by Science Research Associates in Chicago.

One of the games, Collective Bargaining, projects students into a situation aimed at resembling those that shape actual labor-management settlements. The game, which lasts three or four class sessions, involves groups of about six students each. The groups break into two teams; two students represent management and up to four students represent the employes.

Each union team is in competition with all other teams in the class in its effort to obtain the "best" contract, while all management teams compete to settle at lowest cost. Students in each group are asked to assume one of the following roles: plant manager, personnel manager, union business agent, chief steward, or one of several shop stewards.

The performance of each union participant is measured in terms of satisfaction points, which are received in greater or lesser degree for every one of the contract improvements the team is striving for: wage increase, additional holidays, more vacation, higher contributions for insurance, and greater pension benefits. Management's performance is measured in terms of the cost of each item negotiated.

To emphasize the political nature of the conflict and to help provide greater variety, the interests and inclinations of each individual participant differ from those of the others. Even management men see the situation from their own respective points of view, which do not fully agree.

At the beginning of the game, the union teams decide in caucus on their demands, while the management teams deliberate on their strategy. The groups then meet, and each team explains its respective position. Afterwards, the teams huddle to decide on the next steps. Each group appoints a time keeper; if a settlement isn't reached within a specified time, the union is considered to be engaged in a work stoppage and, finally, a strike may occur.

During negotions game administrators record the results of each round. Both sides are penalized by strikes. And since all teams compete against each other, pressure to reach agreement increases as the strike drags on. Gamesters claim the exercise provides a stimulating base for post-game discussions of the history of the labor movement, labor legislation and the principles involved in wage determination.

Other games devised by Rausch have to do with supply and demand, scarcity and allocation, the national economy, banking, international trade and the firm. In the latter game, "students operate a retail store and explore the relationships between costs, profits, assets and liabilities while competing among each other to have the most effective store operation," says Rausch.

Geography is the subject of a panoply of games devised by the High School Geography Project, a Boulder, Colo., group sponsored by the Assn. of American Geographers and funded by the National Science Foundation. One of the Project's most popular exercises is the Game of Section, which mixes politics and geography as high school students assume the parts of legislative representatives from manufacturing, farming, urban and other districts of the hypothetical state of Midland. They are in competition for allocation of state funds.

The game is supposed to illustrate to players how a conflict of interest among the various sections of a political territory is expressed in the political process. Midland is composed of a capital, Centerville, and four sections: an agricultural section, a declining manufacturing section, a growing manufacturing section and an underdeveloped rural section.

Two levels of conflict within Midland are explored in the game. While the sections are competing for public funds for highways, schools and hospitals, individual citizens are competing for the projects that will bring them the greatest personal benefit.

To play the game, the class is divided so that each student can play the part of a particular citizen and be a member of one of the sectional teams. He might be a textile mill owner for the Boomtown section, an unemployed worker from Centerville, a lumberer from the Pleasant Mountain section or the political representative assigned to each section. Students first study role profiles to understand the background and interest of the citizens they are portraying. Then they read the *Midland Gazette* for information on the needs of their section.

The game is staged at a time just prior to the opening of a session of the Midland State Legislature. When the legislature meets, it will allocate funds for public projects on the basis of a budget drawn up by an Executive Committee and the political representatives and approved by a vote of the citizens of Midland. Here is how the game works:[17]

"In the first stage of the game members of each sectional team meet with their political representatives to identify the projects their section needs most. One of the levels of conflict is involved here as the citizens of each argue among themselves and attempt to arrange their requests in some sort of priority order. The factory owners are not going to be interested in the same projects the blue collar citizens of the section will favor. Nor will the lumbering interests want what the sports enthusiasts will favor. But a priority listing must be arrived at, and when it is, the citizens are given an opportunity to communicate with members of other sections in order to define and line up support for mutually beneficial projects.

"The political representatives then meet with the State Executive Committee to draw up a tentative budget. Here the second level of conflict is introduced. Each representative will try to get as many of his section's proposals on the budget as he can. To be effective he will have to convince the committee and the other representatives that each proposal will benefit not only his section but the state as a whole.

"The Executive Committee acts as a moderator and attempts to steer the representatives toward a budget that will be accepable to all the sections."

After the final budget is adopted, the game is halted for evaluation and scoring. The political representatives and the Executive Committee must now face political judgment. Each citizen votes to decide if his representative has upheld his interests and whether he should continue to represent the section. The citizens also vote on whether the Executive Committee has been impartial and should continue in office. Finally, a scoring procedure is used to decide which sectional team did the best job in securing state allocations.

Among other Geography Project games are the Metfab Company Activity, in which students play executives who use data appropriate to their positions (president, treasurer, personnel manager, etc.) to decide where to locate a new metal fabricating plant. In the Game of Farming, players assume the roles of farmers who have migrated to western Kansas. They make decisions about crops to raise and, as a result, end up seeing their incomes either rise or fall.

Teachers and students almost invariably get excited about these and other simulations recently introduced in the classroom. In 1967, Educational Testing Service, Inc., Princeton, N.J., surveyed teachers whose students had played the Game of Section. The ETS report noted, "Over three-fourths of the teachers thought that the activity was extremely effective in helping students to learn." Yet empirical findings on the learning effects of games don't always support the optimists. The question remains whether the exercises are as good as their makers contend.

CHAPTER 7

GAMES: DO THEY MAKE ANY DIFFERENCE?

"A fellow who takes a bull by the tail once gets as much as sixty or seventy times the information as one who doesn't."—*Mark Twain*

Johns Hopkins' Sarane Boocock has identified three phases through which classroom simulation has passed: (1) acceptance on faith — 1962-63; (2) post-honeymoon—1963-65; and (3) realistic optimism — 1965 to present. Even though extreme optimism today is passe among sophisticated gamesters, there remain a few true believers. Typical of the sanguine view is that of Clark Abt:[1]

"Educational games use the student's way of viewing things. They present concrete problems in a simplified but dramatic form that mediates between abstraction and confusion, between dry theory and multi-variably reality. For elementary school children, educational games translate the child's primarily concrete, intuitive thinking into a sequence of dramatized possibilities that expands his awareness of hypothetical alternatives and fundamental relations. The child deeply involved in the concrete activity of educational gaming becomes aware of formal relationships by direct experimental manipulation. Pleasurable rewards for manipulating formal relationships effectively are fed back immediately in the form of game success. Elementary school children tend to focus on only one aspect of a phenomenon at a time, greatly limiting their ability to comprehend phenomena with even a few interactions among elements. Games present simultaneously progressing multiple inter-

actions that can be examined one at a time, and then gradually together with increasing comprehensibility. . . .

"The student player gains a growing sense of structure among the game variables, with a correspondingly growing sense of structure of the subject simulated by the game. This can expand the student's attention span and intellectual confidence. The more densely packed a game is with such structure (up to a surprisingly high degree of apparent confusion), the longer the learning episode that can be tolerated by the student without fatigue or loss of interest. The longer and more concentrated the learning episode, the greater the student's understanding and confidence in the intellectual satisfactions of subsequent episodes."

Many game-makers now believe this unbounded enthusiasm for games is no longer justified. Working with early versions of games developed for the Man: A Course of Study curriculum, two researchers associated with Education Development Center encountered serious problems with the exercises. For one thing, the exercises proved to be "noisy," primarily because of young players' common lack of success in maintaining the appropriate strategic role.[2]

"If in a chemistry class we wanted totally uninitiated children to learn about the properties of acid and base reactions, we wouldn't demonstrate with chemicals which equally naive students had put together," says the two researchers, Marilyn Clayton and Richard Rosenbloom. Granting that when students interact with each other in games they do learn something about human behavior, the two researchers suggest that what youngsters in fact learn is how other school children respond to an unfamiliar situation, not how Netsilik hunters respond to an approaching caribou herd.

It's uncertain, then, whether games always teach what instructors want them to teach. According to Clayton and

Rosenbloom, children become competitive, or bored, but rarely suggest the psychological model of hungry Netsiliks cooperating with each other to catch a caribou to bring home to their families. Consequently, the two researchers aver nothing more is learned than the obvious—that attempts to make students feel lonely, religious or hungry in a game situation are ineffective. They report:

"Further, if a student does successfully perceive the structure of the situation for himself and figures out a good strategy, and if he feels he is really behaving as, for example, a Netsilik would, he may be left with the impression that structure is discovered and strategy worked out anew by each member of a culture. In a conventional game setting it is hard to create an impression of gradual cultural adaptation as knowledge and technique are passed on from one generation to the next." On another occasion these two scholars noted:[8]

"Another related difficulty is that the only kind of reward that can be realistically built into a game situation is maximization of some countable entity, be it money, token food, points or stars. This imposes a very unrealistic picture of psychological motivation in other cultures. . . . Companionship is perhaps as important a factor as the large catch. . . . Students may learn to cooperate in a game to show that cooperation is better than competition, but they are cooperating to maximize an outcome of the game, rather than some inner feeling unconnected with the game.

"And lastly, events of real magnitude such as death, hunger, separation are divorced from emotional consequences and can only be represented in the most artificial way. Ability to test action without consequence may be a real boon to structure and strategy perception but it is not conducive to empathetic insight into the lives of others."

Not surprisingly, critics outside the game world are even more skeptical about the new exercises. Discussing Johns

Hopkins's Game of Legislature, one critic charged that the game presented a gross distortion of the legislative process and "indoctrinated the players into a number of naive misconceptions, especially the impression that legislators get reelected only by satisfying the selfish interests of constituents."[4] He observes that reelection is more related to use of mass media and projection of a winning image than with satisfying the greatest number of voters.

Some critics assail the games on moral grounds. Bernard Cohen, a political scientist at the University of Wisconsin, claims that games may tend to "dehumanize" students by allowing them to maneuver the lives of others without at the same time subjecting players to a system of constraints similar to that which exists in the real world. He notes that the only constraint in many current games is the fear of low marks from the teacher.

Gamesters retort that the exercises aren't supposed to preach. Instead, they insist games teach constructive behavior and attitudes because of their more indirect approach. A Johns Hopkins researcher argues that games implicitly encourage desirable attitudes by making success (or "payoffs") contingent upon "good" behavior.[5]

In the Family Game, for example, youngsters are expected to learn the advantages of compromise between parent and child. How do they learn this? By discovering that if they "hurt" the parents they end up limiting their own "satisfactions" at the same time. As one observer retorts, the child learns to compromise, not because of filial piety or the Golden Rule, but because it is advantageous—it "pays."

This does not, however, answer the big questions: Do students learn more facts from games than from conventional teaching methods? Do strategy games spur critical thinking? Do they really inculcate constructive values? So far there is little evidence to argue one way or the other, particularly as to whether games teach values.

Few critics deny that games spur enthusiasm. But they point out that the few studies that have been made fail to confirm that students learn facts from them that could not have been learned from traditional methods. After evaluating the results of six different studies on the educational impact of such exercises as Life Career, Community Disaster, Inter-Nation Simulation, and others, Cleo H. Cherryholmes, a political scientist at Michigan State University, said his findings were disappointing.

While agreeing that simulations do create more student motivation and interest, he found that they produce no consistent or significant difference in learning, retention, critical thinking or attitude change. He says: "Students do not learn significantly more facts or principles by participating in a simulation than in a more conventional classroom activity."[6]

Even so, Cherryholmes allows that it is "plausible to assume that simulations produce effects that have not been specified and measured" in the studies analyzed. He suggests that more attention should be given the "social-psychological impact" of games, and it is precisely in this area that Johns Hopkins's Sarane Boocock insists games can have a profound effect. To prove it she tested the impact of Life Career and the Game of Legislature on some 1,200 4-H Club delegates attending a national conference. Half the young people were placed in an experimental group that played the games while the other half were part of a control group that did not.

Mrs. Boocock found that participants tended to gain from the legislative game a more realistic view of the pressures on legislators that prevent their acting solely on "principle." Perhaps more important, the "data revealed a trend toward greater feelings of political efficacy" on the part of players after the exercise. Thus, she believes her findings have significance in light of several sociological studies of political behavior, which have shown that the people most likely to take an active part in politics are those with strong feelings of "potency" or efficacy.

"In other words," she declares, "the unique contribution of the simulation experience to feelings of efficacy may be in giving young people the confidence needed to *act* upon the intellectual information they have acquired about a poltical or other situation."[7]

One obvious problem, of course, is how to measure different kinds of learning. The absence of such a technique particularly complicates evaluating the effectiveness of games with normally "unsuccessful" students. In field work with youngsters from a school in a very low income neighborhood, Johns Hopkins researchers observed pupils making very shrewd moves — and making them repeatedly so as to show that they were not simply random or lucky moves.[8]

However, such students were seldom able to explain in words what they did. Bruner also has found that students are often able to perform intellectual tasks requiring the use of abstract rules or theories well before they can say what these rules or theories are. "It can be demonstrated," says Bruner, "that fifth grade children can play mathematical games with rules modeled on highly advanced mathematics; indeed they can arrive at these rules inductively and learn how to work with them. They will flounder, however, if one attempts to force upon them a formal mathematical description of what they have been doing, though they are perfectly capable of guiding their behavior by these rules."

Yet, as Mrs. Boocock observes, the highest order of understanding means not only being able to act effectively but also being able to say what you are doing. "What we wish to make clear here, though, is that these are two distinguishable kinds of performance, and for young people with academic backgrounds of deprivation and failure, the former alone may represent a real intellectual victory," says the researcher. But she notes it may be impossible to test gamesters' belief in the great importance of simulation gaming for the poor school performer without designing some ways to measure different kinds of learning.

There is no question that games, when properly used, can have value. When used in conjunction with other materials, they can provide useful points of departure for discussion. At best, then, games can supplement other educational programs, making real and vivid material that often seems abstract in a textbook. If nothing else, they can convey to the player a feeling for the complexity and multiplicity of factors that must be considered in decision-making. And conceivably they may increase the confidence of young people to deal with real world problems that seem impossibly remote from their own lives.

But the nature of games makes them vulnerable to abuse, particularly in the hands of inexperienced or lazy teachers. Used in isolation from books or discussion groups, the danger arises that games — most of which mirror political and economic institutions as they are — may encourage quiescent and conformist attitudes. In the course of playing, students may hone techniques that enable them to master the game. One may question whether this spurs critical thinking, since success is premised on accepting the "simulated reality" as it is rather than on examining what is wrong with it.

Equally worrisome is the heavy emphasis often placed on winning, which may mislead the player as to the real objectives of learning. One Harvard skeptic wonders if games might not encourage "a feeling that values and principles are merely a set of rules, no better or worse than any set of rules, and the only way of judging between sets of rules is expediency in pursuit of various goals. Winning may become an end in itself."

It is, of course, too early to resolve such reservations and, for that matter, too early to be pessimistic about the newfangled exercises. Whatever the uncertainties that now surround games, some things can be said for certain. The burgeoning market for games reflects further movement away two longtime staples of the classroom: unrealistic and idealized textbook views of American life, and the old teacher-pupil relationship in which the former hands down pronouncements to be regurgitated by the latter. Increasingly the focus is on realism, and increasingly students are expected to learn by themselves. Or at least without the intervention of Gradgrind teachers drilling home facts by slamming rulers on desk tops.

REFERENCES

CHAPTER 1

1. Jeremiah J. O'Connell and Patrick J. Robinson, "Prestige Pays," Working Paper No. 49, Wharton School of Finance and Commerce, University of Pennsylvania, Philadelphia, March, 1967.

2. Sidney F. Giffin, *The Crisis Game*, Doubleday & Co., New York, 1965, p. 9.

3. Giffin, *ibid.*, p. 16. 4. Giffin, *ibid.*, p. 19.

5. James L. McKenney, *Simulation Gaming for Management Development*, monograph published by division of research, Graduate School of Business Administration, Harvard University, 1967. p. 9.

6. McKenney, *ibid.*, p. 9.

7. Clayton J. Thomas, "The Genesis and Practice of Operational Gaming," *Proceedings of the First International Conference on Operational Research* (Baltimore: Operations Research Society of America, 1957), p. 68.

8. *U.S. Naval Institute Proceedings*, March 1964, p. 52.

9. Giffin, *op. cit.*, pp. 46-47.

10. JCS Politico-Military Desk Games, presented by Lt. Col. Thomas J. McDonald, JWGA, Office of the Joint Chiefs of Staff, in *Second War Gaming Symposium Proceedings*, Washington Operations Research Council, March 1964, p. 63.

11. John Deane Potter, Yamamoto, Paperback Library, Inc., New York, 1965, pp. 201-202.

12. Roberta Wohlstetter, *Pearl Harbor: Warning and Decision*, Stanford University Press, 1962, pp. 354-56.

13. James S. Coleman and Sarane S. Boocock, "Games with Simulated Environments in Learning," *Sociology of Education*, Vol. 39, No. 3, Summer, 1966, p. 216.

14. Coleman and Boocock, *ibid.*, p. 217.

15. Coleman and Boocock, *ibid.*, p. 218.

16. Coleman and Boocock, *ibid.*, p. 219.

17. James S. Coleman, *The Adolescent Society*, The Free Press, New York, 1961, p. 309.

18. Coleman, *ibid.*, p. 320. 19. Coleman, *ibid.*, p. 322

20 Johan Huizinga, *Homo Ludens*, Beacon Press, Boston, 1955, p. 211.

21. Paul Pfuetze, *Self, Society, Existence*, Harper Torchbooks, New York, 1954, pp. 87-89.

22. James S. Coleman, In Defense of Games," *American Behavioral Scientist*, October, 1966, p. 3.

23. Frank H. Knight, *Risk, Uncertainty and Profit*, Houghton Miffln Co., Boston & New York, 1921, p. 53.

24. McKenney, *op. cit.*, pp. 4-6 25. McKenney, *op. cit.*, pp. 4-6.

Chapter 2

1. Clark C. Abt, "Games for Learning," *The Social Studies Curriculum Program,* Educational Services, Inc., Cambridge, Mass., 1966, p. 7.

2. Clark C. Abt, "War Gaming," *International Science and Technology,* August, 1964, p. 29.

3. James S. Coleman, "Simulation Games and Social Theory," Occasional Paper, The Center for the Study of Social Organization of Schools, Johns Hopkins University, Baltimore., 1967, p. 2.

4. James L. McKenney, *Simulation Gaming for Management Development,* monograph published by division of research, Graduate School of Business Administration, Harvard University, Cambridge, Mass., 1967, p. 2.

5. McKenney, *ibid.*, p. 42. 6. McKenney, *ibid.*, p. 43.

7. McKenney, *ibid.*, p. 44.

8. James L. McKenney and William R. Dill, "Influences on Learning in Simulation Games," *American Behavioral Scientist,* October, 1966, pp. 28-32.

9. McKenney and Dill, *ibid.*, pp. 28-32.

10. McKenney and Dill, *ibid.*, pp. 28-32.

11. McKenney and Dill, *ibid.*, pp. 28-32.

12. Kalman J. Cohen, William R. Dill. Alfred A. Kuehn, Peter R. Winters, *The Carnegie Tech Management Game,* Richard D. Irwin, Inc., Homewood, Ill., 1964, p. 13.

13. Cohen, et al., ibid., p. 18.

14. Cohen, et al., *ibid.*, p. 21.

15. Cohen, et al., *ibid.*, p. 337.

16. Cohen, et al., *ibid.*, p. 91.

17. Cohen, et al., *ibid.*, p. 93.

18. Cohen, et al., *ibid.*, p. 254.

19. Cohen, et al., *ibid.*, p. 256.

20. Hans B. Thorelli, Robert L. Graves, and Lloyd T. Howells, "The International Operations Simulation at the University of Chicago," *The Journal of Business of the University of Chicago,* July, 1962, p. 287.

21. Hans B. Thorelli and Robert L. Graves, *International Operations Simulation,* The Free Press of Glencoe, New York, N.Y., 1964, p. 11.

22. Thorelli, et al., *op. cit.*, p. 290.

23. Thorelli, et al., *op. cit.*, p. 291.

CHAPTER 3

1. Robert C. Shukraft, "Everything's Up-to-date . . . In Augustine City," *Chimes,* Fall, 1966, p. 3.

2. William James, *Talks to Teachers on Psychology: And to Students on Some of Life's Problems,* Holt, Rinehart and Winston, Inc, New York, 1908, p. 40.

3. Jerome Bruner, *Process of Education,* Harvard University Press, Cambridge, Mass, 1960, p. 81.

4. Chadwick F. Alger, "Use of the Inter-Nation Simulation in Undergraduate Teaching," Simulation in International Relations, Prentice-Hall, Inc., Englewood Cliffs, N.J., 1963, p. 152.

5. Harold Guetzkow, "Simulation in International Relations," from *Proceedings of the IBM Scientific Computing Symposium on Simulation Models and Gaming,* Thomas J. Watson Research Center, Yorktown Heights, N.Y., Dec. 7-9, 1964, p. 250.

6. Richard A. Brody, "Varieties of Simulations in International Relations Research," *Simulation in International Relations,* Prentice-Hall, Inc., Englewood Cliffs, N.J., 1963, p. 197.

7. Harold Guetzkow, "A Use of Simulation in the Study of Inter-Nation Relations," *Simulation in International Relations,* Prentice-Hall, Inc., Englewood Cliffs, N.J., 1963. p. 27.

8. Brody, *op. cit.*, p. 191.

9. Brody, *op. cit*, pp 211-12

10. Guetzkow, "Simulation in International Relations," *op. cit.*, pp. 259-260.

11. Alger, *op. cit.*, pp. 152-53.

12. H. Goldhamer and H. Speier, "Some Observations on Political Gaming," World Politics, XII, 1959, p. 79.

13. Robert C. Noel, "Inter-Nation Simulation Participants' Manual," *Simulation in International Relations,* Prentice-Hall, Inc., Englewood Cliffs, N.J., 1963, p. 44.

14. Noel, *ibid.*, p. 52.

15. Noel, *ibid.*, pp. 59-60.

16. Noel, *ibid.*, pp. 60-61.

17. Alger, *op. cit.*, p. 170.

18. Alger, *op. cit.*, p. 179.

19. Alger, *op. cit.*, p. 162

20. Shukraft, *op. cit.*, p. 3.

21. Shukraft, *op. cit.*, p. 4.

22. Shukraft. *op. cit.*, p. 4.

CHAPTER 4

1. *Germantown Courier,* Nov. 23, 1967, p. 3.

2. *Newsweek,* Jan. 15, 1968, p. 51.

3. "Simulation Games for the Social Studies Classroom," *New Dimensions,* Vol. 1, No. 1, Foreign Policy Association, New York, 1968, p. 14.

4. Crisis Teacher's Guide, Western Behavioral Sciences Institute, La Jolla, Calif., 1966, p. 3.

CHAPTER 5

1. James S. Coleman and Sarane Boocock, "Games with Simulated Environments in Learning," *Sociology of Education,* Vol. 39, No. 3, Summer, 1966, p. 221.

2. Gerald Zaltman, "Degree of Participation and Learning in a Consumer Economics Game," *Simulation Games in Learning,* Sage Publications, Beverly Hills, Calif., 1968, p. 2.

3. Sarane Boocock, "Innovation in the Social Studies: Prospects and Problems," speech delivered at Fall Conference of the Pennsylvania Council for the Social Studies, Sept. 23, 1967, p. 11.

4. Boocock, *ibid.*, p. 11.

5. Sarane Boocock, "Simulation of a Learning Environment for Career Planning and Vocational Choice," revised version of papers delivered before annual meetings of American Personnel and Guidance Assn., April, 1966, and American Psychological Assn., September, 1966, p. 3.

6. Barbara Varenhorst, "The Life Career Game as a Tool for More Effective Decision-Making Guidance," unpublished paper, Palo Alto, Calif., Unified School District, Fall, 1967, p. 3.

7. Varenhorst, *ibid.*, p. 5.

8. "Simulation Games for the Social Studies Classroom." *New Dimensions*, Vol. 1, No. 1, Foreign Policy Assocaition, New York, 1968, p. 30.

9. Dale C. Farran, "The Effects of Hopkins Simulations on Underachieving 8th Grade Boys," *Simulation Games in Learning*, Sage Publications, Inc., Beverly Hills, Calif., 1968, p. 4.

10. Farran, *ibid.*, p. 7.

11. Farran, *ibid.*, pp. 8-10

12. Farran, *ibid.*, p. 12.

13. Farran, *ibid.*, p. 19.

14. Farran, *ibid.*, p. 21.

15. *New Dimensions, op. cit.*, pp. 10-13.

16. James S. Coleman. "Simulation Games and Social Theory," *Simulation Games in Learning*, Sage Publications, Inc., Beverly Hills, Calif., 1968, p. 3.

17. Coleman, *ibid.*, p. 11-12.

CHAPTER 6

1. Sarane S. Boocock, "Innovation in the Social Studies: Prospects and Problems," September, 1967, p. 2.

2. Jerome S. Bruner, *Toward a Theory of Instruction*, the Belknap Press of Harvard University Press, Cambridge, Mass., 1966, p. 118.

3. Bruner, *ibid.*, p. 74.

4. Bruner, *ibid.*, p. 95.

5. Peter B. Dow, "Man: A Course of Study Reexamined," *Man: A Course of Study*, Education Development Center, Inc., Cambridge, Mass., 1967, p. 61.

6. Dow, *ibid.*, p. 63.

7. J. M. Leonard and R. L. Wing, "Advantages of Using a Computer in Some Kinds of Educational Games," *Human Factors in Electronics*, June, 1967, p. 76.

8. Bruse Moncreiff, excerpts from article in *Programmed Instruction*, Vol. IV, No. 5, February, 1965, pp. 10-11.

9. Moncreiff, *ibid.*

10. Richard L. Wing, *Use of Technical Media for Simulating Environments to Provide Individualized Instruction*, Board of Cooperative Educational Services, Westchester County, N.Y., 1965, p. II, H, 7.

11. Wing, *ibid.*, p. II, H, 11.

12. David Yount and Paul DeKock, "Simulations and the Social Studies," *Innovations in the Social Studies: Teachers Speak for Themselves*, ed., Dale Brubaker, Crowell, Inc., New York, 1968, pp. 1-6.

13. Yount and DeKock, *Ibid.*

14. Yount and Dekock, *ibid.*

15. Yount and DeKock, *ibid.*

16. Peter Wolff, *The Game of Empire,* Occasional Paper No. 9. The Social Studies Curriculum Program Educational Services, Inc., Cambridge. Mass., 1966, p. 8.

17. See *New Dimensions, ibid.*

CHAPTER 7

1. Clark C. Abt, *Games for Learning,* Occasional Paper No. 7, The Social Studies Curriculum Program, Educational Services, Inc., Cambridge, Mass., 1965, pp. 20-21.

2. Marilyn Clayton and Richard Rosenbloom, "Goals and Design: Games in a New Social Studies Course," *Simulation Games In Learning,* Sage Publications, Inc., Beverly Hills, Calif., 1968, pp. 89-90.

3. Clayton and Rosenbloom, *ibid.,* pp. 91-92.

4. Ivor Kraft, "Opinions Differ: Pedagogical Futility in Fun and Games," *NEA Journal,* LVI, January, 1967, pp 71-72.

5. "Simulation Games for the Social Studies Classroom," *New Dimensions,* p. 43.

6. Cleo H. Cherryholmes, "Some Current Research on Effectiveness of Educational Simulations: Implications for Alternative Strategies," *American Behavioral Scientist,* October, 1966, pp. 4-7.

7. Sarane S. Boocock, "An Experimental Study of the Learning Effects of Two Games with Simulated Environments," *American Behavioral Scientist,* October, 1966, pp. 8-17.

8. Sarane S. Boocock, "Innovation in the Social Studies: Prospects and Problems," p. 17.

9. Jerome S. Bruner, *The Process of Education,* Harvard University Press, Cambridge, Mass., 1960, p. 40.

INDEX